Battles of Stirling's Plantation and Bayou Bourbeau

The Fall 1863 Campaign in Louisiana & Texas

Michael Dan Jones

Cover photo: Pvt. Simeon J. Crews, Co. F, 7th Texas Cavalry (Liljenquist Family Collection, Library of Congress).

Copyright © 2015 Michael Dan Jones

All rights reserved.

ISBN-13: 978-1517002176

DEDICATION

This book is respectfully dedicated to the memory of privates Solomon Jones, Nicolas Kibodeaux and Clairville Kibodeaux, all of Company E, 11th Battalion (Spaight's) Texas Volunteer Infantry—the great-great-grandfather and great-great-great uncles of Michael Dan Jones, respectively. And to the memory of Private Samuel D. Jones, of Company E, 11th Texas Infantry Regiment, also the great-great-grandfather of the author.

CONTENTS

	Preface	i
1	Build up for invasion	9
2	The Battle of Stirling's Plantation	17
3	Clashes in Acadiana	34
4	Battle of Bayou Bourbeau	49
5	Fighting Retreat	75
6	Rio Grande Expedition	86
	Appendix I Summary of principal events in the Fall Campaign of 1863	116
	Appendix II Organizations of Armies	120
	Bibliography	127
	Index	130

ALSO BY MICHAEL DAN JONES

1ˢᵗ Louisiana Zouaves: Jeff Davis' Pet Wolves

The Battle of Chickasaw Bayou: A Confederate Victory in the Vicksburg Campaign

9ₜₕ Battalion Louisiana Infantry In the Battle of Baton Rouge and the Siege of Port Hudson.

The Vicksburg 28th Louisiana Infantry.

Lee's Foreign Legion: A History of the 10th Louisiana Infantry, co-author, Tom Brooks.

The Tiger Rifles: The Making of a Louisiana Legend.

General Mouton's Regiment: The 18th Louisiana Infantry.

The Battle of Calcasieu Pass and the Great Naval Raid on Lake Charles, Louisiana.

Dick Dowling and the Jefferson Davis Guard.

The Confederate Cookbook: Delicious Recipes from the Deep South (editor).

A Defense of General Lee (editor).

PREFACE

The Battle of Stirling's Plantation and the Battle of Bayou Bourbeau were the beginning and end of the Fall 1863 Campaign in South Louisiana. Also called the "Great Texas Overland Expedition," it was a failed attempt by the Federal Army of Major General Nathaniel Prentice Banks to invade Texas by way of the Southwest Louisiana bayous and prairies. His Army of the Gulf vastly outnumbered Confederate Major General Richard Taylor's Army of Western Louisiana, which was made up of Louisianians and Texans. For the Louisiana troops, it was a matter of defending their own homes and families. For the Texans, it was a matter of preventing the Northern invaders from reaching their homes and families and wreaking the same kind of devastation that had been done to their Louisiana neighbors. The failure of the Louisiana campaign led directly to the Rio Grande Expedition in Texas.

Banks was under a great deal of pressure from the Lincoln administration to restore Federal control of Texas. Abraham Lincoln was concerned about French activity in Mexico and the serious leak in the blockade of the Southern Republic along the uncontrolled border south of the Rio Grande. Federals had tried to invade Texas for the first time in October, 1862 when a naval expedition successfully captured Galveston without a fight. But the navy didn't bring enough foot soldiers to hold it, and a counterattack led by Confederate Major General John Bankhead Magruder liberated the coastal port town on January 1, 1863. Then, on September 8, 1863, Banks tried again to invade the Lone Star State via Sabine Pass. With four shallow draft gunboats, numerous transports and a 5,000 man U.S. Army contingent, it seemed like a Northern victory would be certain. But 47 scrappy Irish-Texans of Company F, 1st Texas Heavy Artillery under the command of 1st Lieutenant Dick Dowling astounded the world with a signal victory over the invasion force.

Banks, a controversial political general, actually wanted to mount an expedition to Mobile, Alabama to build on his victory in the Siege of Port Hudson, Louisiana that summer. That success helped revive Banks' tarnished military reputation following his embarrassing defeat by Confederate General Stonewall Jackson in the Shenandoah Valley Campaign of 1862. Mobile would actually have been a target with more military significance at that time. But Lincoln was more interested in bringing Texas back under Federal political dominance, so Texas it would be. Banks' superior officer, Major General Henry Wager Halleck, sent the orders and the campaign was soon underway. In the official records of the War of the Rebellion, it is called the "Operations in the Teche Country, La.," October 3-November 30, 1863. But the Fall Campaign really began with September 29 at Stirling's Plantation near Morganza, Louisiana, which was a small but sharp battle that was a complete Confederate victory, as was Bayou Bourbeau. That campaign exhibited the fighting qualities of Trans-Mississippi Confederates, and on the Northern side, the folly of putting an unqualified politicians at the head of one of the major armies on the United States.

Michael Dan Jones

1 BUILDUP FOR INVASION

Maj. Gen. N.P. Banks
(Library of Congress)

Major General Nathaniel Prentice Banks, commander of the Army of the Gulf, received his marching orders for Texas on August 15, 1863. ". . . I made immediate preparations for a movement by the coast against Houston, selecting the position occupied by the enemy on the Sabine as the point of attack," Banks said. "The occupation of Houston would place in our hands the control of all the railway communications of Texas; give us command of the most populous and productive part of the State; enable us to move at any moment into the interior in any direction, or to fall back upon the Island of Galveston, which could be maintained with a very small force, holding the enemy upon the coast of Texas, and leaving the Army of the Gulf free to move upon Mobile, in accordance with my original plan or whenever it should be required." But when his initial invasion was thwarted September 8, 1863 by Dick Dowling and the Jeff Davis Guard, he had to go back to the drawing board.[1]

"I then endeavored, without delay, to carry out my instructions by a

---

[1] *War of the Rebellion: A Compilation of the Union and Confederate Armies* (1880-1901); Series 1, Vol. 26, Pt. 2, P. 19.. Hereafter cited as *O.R.* Unless otherwise cited, all references will be to Series 1.

movement toward Alexandria and Shreveport, or, if possible, across the southern part of Louisiana to Niblett's Bluff," Banks explained. The obstacles he would face on the overland route of Southwest Louisiana were both geographical as well as military. The country from Bayou Teche and the Sabine River was thinly populated by Louisiana Acadians and Anglo-Celtic ranchers and farmers. The main route was over the Old Spanish Trail and the population of the region was too sparse for a large army to live off the land, and too far away from the coast to be resupplied by the navy. "A movement in the direction of Alexandria and Shreveport was equally impracticable," Banks said. It is obvious that the Yankee commander did not have his heart in the overland route, and was just going through the motions to satisfy the insistent Lincoln government.[2]

Banks put Major General William B. Franklin, commander of the 19th Army Corps, in charge of his next effort. This was the same officer who failed at Sabine Pass. In addition, Major General E.O.C. Ord, commanding the 13th Army Corps would supply some of his divisions. When Ord became sick, Major General Cadwallader C. Washburn led the 13th Corps. Franklin had the 1st Division under Brigadier General Godfrey Weitzel and the 3rd Division of Brigadier General Cuvier Grover. The Federal cavalry division was commanded by Brigadier General Albert Lee. There was also a contingent of engineers and unattached units. Subsequent events showed that the troops had little respect for the leadership of the army.

THE SETTING

Confederate Major General Richard Taylor gave a good description of the Acadian culture, as it then existed, in his memoir, *Destruction and Reconstruction*. "The upper or northern Teche waters the parishes of St. Landry, Lafayette, and St. Martin's—the Attakapas, home of the 'Acadians.' What the gentle, contented creole was to the restless, pushing American, that and more was the Acadian to the creole. In the middle of the past century, when the victories of Wolfe and Amherst deprived France of her Northern possessions, the inhabitants of *Nouvelle Acadie*, the present Nova Scotia, migrated to the genial clime of the Attakapas, where beneath the flag of the lilies they could preserve their allegiance, their traditions, and their faith. Isolated up to the time of the war, they spoke no language but their own *patois*; and, reading and writing not having come to them by nature, they were dependent for news on their *curés* and occasional peddlers, who tempted the women with *chiffons* and trinkets.

---

[2] Ibid, Vo. 26, Pt. 1, 20.

"The few slaves owned were humble members of the household, assisting in the cultivation of small patches of maize, sweet potatoes, and cotton, from which last the women manufactured the wonderful Attakapas *cotonnade*, the ordinary clothing of both sexes. Their little *cabanes* dotted the broad prairie in all directions, and it was pleasant to see the smoke curling from their chimneys, while herds of cattle and ponies grazed at will. Here, unchanged, was the French peasant of Fénelon and Bossuet, of Louis le Grand and his successor le Bien-Aimé. Tender and true were his traditions of la belle France, but of France before Voltaire and the encyclopædists, the Convention and the Jacobins—ere she had lost faith in all things, divine and human, save the *bourgeoisie* and *avocats*. Mounted on his pony, with lariat in hand, he herded his cattle, or shot and fished; but so gentle was his nature, that lariat and rifle seemed transformed into pipe and crook of shepherd. Light wines from the Médoc, native oranges, and home-made sweet cakes filled his largest conceptions of feasts; and violin and clarionet made high carnival in his heart," Taylor wrote.[3]

Maj. Gen Richard Taylor
(Copy print, author's collection)

After seizing New Orleans, the Yankee invaders pushed out west of the city driving the small Confederate garrison under Brigadier General Alfred Mouton from Bayou Lafourche. They then set up a massive supply depot across Berwick Bay, in St. Mary Parish at Brashear City, modern day Morgan City. After relieving "Beast" Butler in December, 1862, Banks mounted the first Teche Campaign in the Spring of 1863 and pushed Taylor's small Army of Western Louisiana all the way back to Alexandria—175 miles from Brashear City—and then besieged Port Hudson on the Mississippi May to July. While the siege was going on Taylor temporarily took Brashear City—and captured a mountain of badly needed arms and supplies—before the

---

[3] Richard Taylor, *Destruction and Reconstruction: Personal Experiences of the Late War* (D. Appleton and Co., New York, 1879) 105, 106.

Yankee's returned. By that fall, with the Great Texas Overland Expedition in the offing, Taylor received reinforcements in the form of Major General John G. Walker's Texas Infantry Division, soon to earn the nickname "Greyhounds" for its epic long marches. With Brigadier General Thomas Green's Texas Cavalry Division and Mouton's Louisiana Infantry Brigade, Taylor was in much better shape than he was for the earlier campaigns.

Taylor noted that Walker was a first rate infantry commander. He wrote, "Released at length from the swamps of the Tensas, where it had suffered from sickness, Walker's division of Texas infantry joined me in the early autumn, and was posted to the north of Opelousas. Major-General J.G. Walker served as a captain of mounted rifles in the war with Mexico. Resigning from the United States army to join the Confederacy, he commanded a division at the capture of Harper's Ferry in 1862, and in the subsequent battle of Antietam; after which he was transferred to Arkansas. Seconded by good brigade and regimental officers, he had thoroughly disciplined his men, and made them in every sense soldiers; and their efficiency in action was soon established." [4]

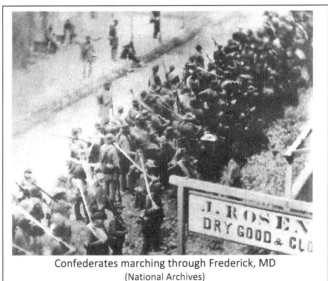
Confederates marching through Frederick, MD
(National Archives)

---

[4] Taylor, 150.

Banks also received major reinforcements, after the Vicksburg Campaign, from the 13th Army Corps. Banks, in September, also ordered "able bodied men of color between twenty and thirty" to either work on government or private plantations, or be enrolled into the *Corps d' Afrique*. By October he had 20 infantry regiments in that command under Brigadier General Daniel Ullmann. They were organized in four brigades in two divisions. The men were far from combat ready and were used mainly for guarding plantations and Forts Jackson and St. Philip on the lower Mississippi. These poorly disciplined troops would engage in looting and other depredations in areas where they were stationed.[5]

Among the reinforcements coming down from Vicksburg with the 13th Army Corps was the 67th Indiana Infantry. The historian of the regiment, Reuben B. Scott, noted they received a brief respite from campaigning when they arrived near New Orleans at the end of August. He wrote, "We were now near the city, and we round in and land at Carlton [Carrollton], some twelve miles above, and we are not permitted now to go down to the city, but go in camp on a beautiful grassy plain just below this little suburban village, and after we had well established ourselves in camp and had washed the dust and smoke from our faces and shaved — those who had beard to shave — and donned our dress suits, we went forth to take in the city, and here we found, built of huge stones, the great custom house, which, by its own weight, had sunken one story beneath the surface; then a little further on we find Jackson's statue, in all his rigid grandeur sitting upon his fiery steed; and then we come to the historic French Market, where we find all peoples, tongues and nationalities. In this market we can find anything that grows in tropical America." It would be a long time before they would have another such enjoyable outing.[6]

One of the Texans, Captain George W. O'Bryan of Beaumont, had been campaigning in Louisiana since May. He was the commander of Company E, 11th Battalion (Spaight's) Texas Volunteers. The battalion had an unusual makeup: companies A and F were cavalry; companies C, D and E, infantry; and Company B, artillery. They had seen combat in Texas in the First Battle of Sabine Pass, September 20, 1862, and in the capture of two Federal gunboats off Sabine Pass on January 20, 1863, during which they served as sea-going marines on a Confederate gunboat. But the campaigning had been taking its toll on his men. O'Bryan's 18-year-old brother-in-law, Private Henry Rowley of his company, became critically ill

---

[5] John D. Winters, *The Civil War in Louisiana* (Louisiana State University Press, Baton Rouge and London, 1963) 312-314.

[6] Reuben S. Scott, *The History of the 67th Regiment Indiana Infantry Volunteers, War of the Rebellion*, Herald Book and Job Print, Bedford, Ind., 1892) 45.

in their camp on the Atchafalaya River, when they got marching orders. He wrote in his diary, dated September 19, "At 10 A.M. the aspect of things was changed to one of cheerful bustle and activity, by the announcement of an order to march westwardly toward Washington [Louisiana] at 1 P.M. precisely. The necessary dispositions were hastily made. The one which

pained me most was the absolute necessity that Henry [Rowley] should be left behind. This morning early he appeared to be improving but when I went to bid the poor fellow Goodbye thinking perhaps of the uncertainty of his fate (his probable capture by the enemy if he should be so fortunate to recover) and the possibility that he might never again be permitted to see the 'loved ones at home,' he manifested by a copious flood of tears the depth of his sorrow, but appeared afterwards to be much relieved and promised me that he would not be any more excited. I endeavored, without meeting with success, to obtain permission of Cols. Harrison & Spaight to leave him one of his acquaintances of the company as a nurse, left him $50, secured him the attention of Capt. [Walthall] Burton and sorrowfully left without the consolation of the hope that I should ever meet him again on Earth." But after marching a day and a half, they were ordered to reverse course and head back to their camp on the Atchafalaya near Morgan's ferry. The marching orders for O'Bryan[7] and his men marked the opening of the Fall Campaign for them.[8]

O'Bryan found his brother-in-law still critically ill. He jotted in his diary on September 21, "The Dr. thinks his disease (diarrhea) will assume a chronic form, but that there is little hope of his perfect recovery. He is very cross and wants me by him all the while." But his young brother-in-law's condition continued to worsen. The infantry captain was absorbed in the suffering of his kinsman until September 26, when the teenage soldier took his last breath. O'Bryan wrote, "He died slowly and like the glimmering extinguishment of an expiring lamp until 5 P.M., when his soul deserted its clayey tenement of sorrow and pain. May God grant for him a happy place in eternity—he died with his hands clasped in mine and tears would flow at the thought of how dear he was to one, to me the dearest thing on earth. He was with the assistance of his friends and fellow soldiers then clothed in his last earthly habiliments, and on Sept. 27 was followed by a concourse of the same to the grave where he was buried with the martial honor due a private in the Army of the Confederate States. The inscription on his head board is, Henry Rowley, a private of Co. E, Spaight's Batn., T.V.I., age 18

---

[7] He changed the spelling on his name from O'Bryan to O'Brien after the war.
[8] Texas State Historical Association. *The Southwestern Historical Quarterly, Volume 67, July 1963 - April, 1964*, H. Bailey Carroll, editor, Journal/Magazine/Newsletter, 1964; (http://texashistory.unt.edu/ark:/67531/metapth101197/ : accessed September 05, 2015), University of North Texas Libraries, The Portal to Texas History, http://texashistory.unt.edu; crediting Texas State Historical Association, Denton, Texas. Cited hereafter, O'Brien Journal.)

years, died Sept. 26th, A.D. 1863."[9]

The activity among the Confederates was in direct response to Federal movements. While Banks was assembling his men, Major General Ulysses S. Grant in Vicksburg sent the 2,500 man division of Major General Francis J. Herron to Morganza, Louisiana to deal with the Confederates on the Atchafalaya. Due to illness, Herron's Division would be led in the coming battle by Major General Napoleon J.T. Dana. A provisional brigade of about 1,000 men was sent out in advance under the command of Colonel J.B. Leake. The force included the 19th Iowa Infantry under the command of Captain William Adams; the 26th Indiana Infantry under Colonel A.D. Rose, one section of the 1st Missouri Light Artillery, the 6th Missouri Cavalry Battalion, Battery E under the command of Major Samuel Montgomery and the 2nd Illinois Cavalry. There was also a company of mounted infantry under Lieutenant Henry Walton of the 34th Iowa. The stage was now set for the first battle of the Fall Campaign.[10]

---

[9] O'Brien Journal, 53,54.
[10] Winters, 296. O.R., Vol. 26 Pt. 1, 322, 323.

2 THE BATTLE OF STIRLING'S PLANTATION

The skirmishing began on September 7 at Morgan's Ferry on the Atchafalaya and continued, off and on, up to the Battle of Stirling's Plantation on September 29. Captain O'Bryan's company, with Spaight's Battalion, was sent to the Atchafalaya as reinforcements in direct response to the enemy activity.

The Battle of Stirling's Plantation—also known as Sterling's Plantation, Fordoche Bridge and Bayou Fordoche—was a precursor of the Great Texas Overland Expedition. It showed both the vulnerability of the large, widespread Federal forces, and the fighting capabilities of the Confederate forces. General Dana didn't take command of the operation until September 28 after the various dispositions had been made. Leake's detachment was seven miles below the town of Morganza, the main Federal base of operations. "Lieutenant-Colonel Leake's instructions from Major-General Herron were to keep the country well reconnoitered; to keep his cavalry constantly out; to push daily reconnaissance parties toward the Atchafalaya, where a considerable force of the enemy were posted, and frequently to

Maj. Gen. N.J.T. Dana
(Library of Congress)

push his advances up the river, and annoy the enemy's pickets and drive them in. The morning after I assumed command (yesterday), I dispatched a courier with an escort to Lieutenant-Colonel Leake, with orders, &c.; two wagons loaded with knapsacks belonging to his command were sent out with a small infantry guard."[11]

In response, on September 9, Captain O'Bryan wrote in his diary, "Marched 12 miles to Bayou Bouef 4 miles above Washington; received intelligence that the enemy was advancing on Col. Green on Atchafalaya—hastening on." They marched 18 miles the next day, September 10, and then eight miles the next day and reached the main encampment at Morgan's Ferry. Then on September 13, he wrote, "Our pickets on the other side driven in—all bustle and preparation for fight, wagons and sick sent to the rear, resulting in an artillery duel on our right accompanied with lively sharp-shooting. Nobody hurt on our side."[12]

An unidentified Federal sergeant.
(CDV, author's collection)

Colonel Leake originally made his headquarters at the Norwood Plantation, but soon realized that the local road system made him very vulnerable to attack. He requested and received permission to move his headquarters back to the Stirling Plantation, where he thought he would be more secure. He positioned his forces in and around the various outbuildings, include the negro quarters, sugar house and other structures. He also posted pickets as advantageously as he could.

---

[11] O.R., Vol. 26, Pt. 1, 322.
[12] O'Brien Journal, 49, 50.

One of the soldiers of the 19th Iowa wrote later that the men thought Leake overly strict on the pickets—a concern which proved to be unfounded. Leake was learning that there was a large force of Rebels in his rear, which only increased his sense of vulnerability.[13]

Private James Irvine Dungan of Company C, 19th Iowa, was the post-war historian of the regiment. He wrote, "It seems to be the impression that we were *surprised!* far from it; for to be surprised is to be taken off your guard, when unprepared and unexpected. It means a want of vigilance and fore-sight; it means that duty has been neglected in some particular, and in none of these things were we surprised. Our pickets saw the advancing skirmish line of the enemy; our pickets fired the *first* shots, and the rebels had only replied by a few shots, when the 19th was in line; and our regiment delivered the *first* volley of the fight."

CONFEDERATE ADVANCE

With the Federals becoming increasingly active, General Taylor ordered an attack on the Federals around Stirling's Plantation. General Mouton, on September 19, ordered General Green to prepare to advance on the Federals, with orders to attack issued September 25. The infantry assembled were Mouton's Louisisana Brigade, commanded by Colonel Henry Gray, and Speight's Texas Infantry Brigade, which was then under the command Lieutenant Colonel James E. Harrison. Mouton's Brigade at the time included the 18th Louisiana Infantry, commanded by Colonel Leopold Armant; 24th Louisiana Infantry (also called the Crescent Regiment), commanded by Colonel Abel Bosworth; 28th Louisiana (Gray's) Louisiana Infantry, Lieutenant Colonel William Walker; and the infantry battalions of the 10th Louisiana, Colonel Valsin A. Fournet; 11th Louisiana, Colonel James H. Beard; and the 12th/16th Louisiana, Lieutenant Colonel Franklin H. Clack. Speight's/Harrison's Texas Brigade was made up of the 11th Battalion (Spaight's) Texas Volunteers, infantry companies C, D and E, commanded by Lieutenant Colonel Ashley W. Spaight; the 15th Texas Infantry, Major John W. Daniel; and 31st Texas (Hawpe's) Texas Cavalry (Dismounted), Major Frederick J. Malone. A 15 man detachment of Waller's Cavalry Battalion, under Lieutenant R.N. Weisiger, accompanied the infantry.[14]

The mounted element included the 13th (Waller's) Texas Cavalry Battalion, under command of Major Hannibal H. Boone; Major Lee C.

---

[13] J. Irvine Dungan, *History of the Nineteenth Regiment Iowa Volunteer Infantry* (Luse & Griggs, Davenport, Iowa, 1865) 84-89.

[14] O.R., Vol. 26, Pt. 1, 332. O'Bryan Journal, 236.

Rountree's Texas Cavalry Battalion; 3rd Cavalry Regiment, Arizona Brigade, Colonel George T. Madison, and the 4, 5th and 7th Texas Cavalry (dismounted), took part in the operation. Also sent was the 1st Confederate (Semmes') Artillery, but almost constant rain greatly hampered the movement of the guns. The Federals estimated the Confederate force at 5,000, but that is probably an over-estimate. It was more likely around 3,000—plus or minus. However about the same number on each side were actually engaged in the fighting.

Many Texas Confederates wore black hats and homespun uniforms, similar to the above Confederate infantryman.
(Liljenquist Collection, Library of Congress)

General Tom Green, a legendary cavalryman and hero of the Texas Revolution, Mexican War, and now the War for Southern Independence, was put in overall command of the assault by Mouton, who was his senior in rank. Green sent out an order at midnight on September 26 for Colonel James P. Major, commanding Major's Cavalry Brigade, to send out his best regiment to Lyons' Ferry on the Atchafalaya, to cross the ferry, march to Livonia and by the night of the 28th and morning of the 29th, to move up to the Fordoche Bridge near Morganza. Major assigned that mission to the 3rd Cavalry Regiment, Arizona Brigade. Green then, on the 27th, had assembled two ferry flatboats that could transport as many as 18 horses or 80 footmen at a time. He then assembled all his force and at 3 o'clock on the afternoon of the 28th, commenced crossing the Atchafalaya River. First, Speight's and Mouton's brigades crossed; then the 4th, 5th and 7th Texas Cavalry regiments. The operation was completed by 1 a.m. the 29th, and at daylight they began the March to Bayou Fordoche. They followed a trail 4 miles through the swamp to its intersection with the state road to Morganza, which would take them to Mrs. Mary Stirling's Plantation on the eastside of Bayou Fordoche.[15]

Green ordered the infantry to attack the Federals from the north, while Rountree's and Waller's horse soldiers would attack from the south. The Confederate cavalry were wearing blue uniforms that had been captured at the great Federal supply depot in June at Brashear City.

Captain O'Bryan of Spaight's Battalion recorded the march in detail in his diary. He wrote, "Tuesday at sunrise—Counter marched to the ferry and proceeding up the river through an interminable cocklebur patch about a mile, thence eastwardly, held eastwardly and crookedly along a path wide enough for one man, about 6 miles we emerged into the Morganza road between the enemy and their support (if any) at the latter place." At that time, Mouton's Brigade, which had been in the lead, stepped to the side of the road and let Speight's Brigade go into the lead. O'Bryan continued, "This point was distant from Morganza 5 miles. We [Speight's Brigade] were ordered to enter the cane field across a levee and forming immediately after in column to advance up the enemy while Mouton's Brig. was held in reserve. I enquired of Lt. Col. Spaight where the enemy was and was answered that he was directly in front."[16]

On the Federal side, Colonel Leake was thoroughly alarmed by the increasing rebel presence in this rear, to the west of Bayou Fordoche. He had a gap dug in the levee along the bayou, in front of Mrs. Stirling's house, so the section of 1st Missouri Light Artillery could sweep the cane field in as their front. He also had a breast work dug to the north of the house, as well and men stationed in and around the out buildings. The Federal 6th Missouri Cavalry camp was to the south of the house. Dungan, in his regimental history of the 19th Iowa, was understandably defensive about their conduct. He wrote, "Then we were *not* surprised in the attack, but there was that to surprise in the defense, that four hundred and fifty men should hold at bay over *five* thousand for two hours and ten minutes by the watch, was surprising." Besides the 19th Iowa, Leake also had the 26th Indiana, as well as cavalry and artillery to back him up—nearly 1,000 men to defend the position. For some unknown reason, the Federal artillery was

---

[15] O.R., Vol. 26, Pt. 1, 329, 330.
[16] O'Brien Journal, 236, 237.

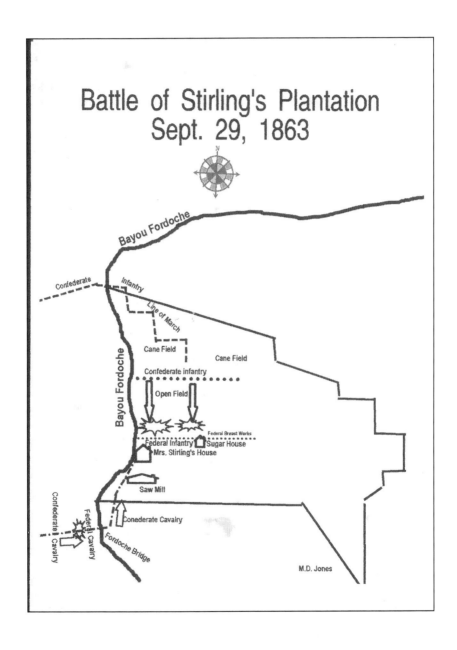

never put in the gap. The guns were kept among the buildings where they were of little use.[17]

The advance Confederate cavalry reached the Fordoche Bridge, about a mile below Mrs. Stirling's house, which was named Botany Bay, and opened fire on the Yankee pickets at about 11 o'clock. They skirmished a half-hour before the dismounted cavalry arrived. General Green said he deployed one section of Semmes' Battery, under the command of Lieutenant J.A.A. West, supported by the 4th and 5th Texas, in a plowed field and then opened fire on the enemy. He also ordered another two sections of artillery, with Major Boone's (Waller's) 13th Texas, and the 7th Texas, to move rapidly to the bridge. He added, ". . . the dismounted men of the Fourth and Fifth moving at a double-quick across the plowed field to the quarters, but the enemy's advance of cavalry had fallen back to their headquarters, 1 mile farther on, at a Mr. Norwood's house. The sections of artillery united at the bridge and the whole command proceeded with great rapidity toward the house. Majors Boone and Rountree made a dashing charge upon the enemy's cavalry, drawn up in line of battle near the house, and scattered them with such effect that they were not seen afterward, having retreated through a lane and turn rows to a road leading around the rear of plantations, which was unknown to me."[18]

GEN. TOM GREEN, C.S.A.
(Copy Print)

(*Six Decades in Texas*)

Green went on to say, "During these transactions, the firing from the rear had continued with slight interruption, and Major Boone was ordered to take his own command and Rountree's battalion and charge the enemy at Mrs. Stirling's, which he did most gallantly, charging the enemy's battery and receiving severe wounds. This charge closed the fight, the enemy surrendering in detachments as they retreated and were overtaken by our troops."

Meanwhile, on the other-side of the plantation, the main infantry attack was taking place by Speight's Texas Brigade with Clack's 12th Louisiana from Mouton's Brigade reinforcing the Texans. The rest of

---

[17] Dungan, 89.
[18] O.R. Vol. 26, Pt. 1, 329.

Mouton's Brigade was in reserve. With the 15th Texas Infantry in the lead, the foot soldiers crossed the levee and entered a cane field, moving through the rows of growing vegetation, which obscured their view of the enemy position. The Yankees, however, detected the rebels coming at them through the cane and opened fire. The Confederates were zig-zagging through the field when the bullets began whizzing past them. They then had to cross and open field to charge the enemy position. Colonel Harrison, commanding Speight's Brigade, wrote, "The advance upon his [the Federal] position was compelled to be through an open field; some four hundred yards through appalling fire from his Entire force. He Enfiladed me by occupying with a portion of his forces a large Sugar Mill and building connected with them. I detached a portion of my command [Spaight's Battalion] and dislodged them, and with the same detachment attacked his flank forcing him to abandon his first position and Change his front."[19]

Captain O'Bryan of Spaight's Battalion gave a more detailed account of the charge in his diary. He wrote, while going through the cane field, "We proceeded then 2 or 300 yds. to a turning row, field to the right, to the left and to the right again for a distance of 1-1½ miles on the *qui vive* all the while for the enemy. When along the turning row we had arrived within 3 or 400 yards of a large sugar house in sight we filed to the right down the cane rows under considerable fire, and when Clack's Batn. on the left were covered by the cane, without halting or fronting, the command to forward and to charge, with an occasional cry to retreat, were commingled together in dreadful confusion, while the enemy rained among us and the cane around us a terrible shower of whistling wounding and killing bullets.

Capt. George W. O'Bryan, Co. E. 11th Bn. Tex. Vol. Inf.
(Copy print, author's collection)

"After some hesitation in consequence of the want of order and deliberation in our comdr., the natural bravery of the troops induced them, with the example of the more daring and gallant, to front and advance toward the enemy whence the firing proceeded. Advancing a short distance

---

[19] Alwynn Barr, *Polignac's Texas Brigade* (Texas A&M University Press, College Station, 1998), 26.

we arrived at a ditch where another halt was voluntarily made, owing to the security offered by the ditch against the whirlwind of bullets around us. The command to Fire was given, heard, and the entire line discharged their pieces with very little, if any, effect from the fact that the cane was so high that the enemy or his position could not be seen. It was heard that Maj. [Josephus S.] Irvine's son, Patton, was killed by a Minnie ball through the breast, also that Robt. Burrell received a severe wound in the leg. Hearing along the line the cry of Charge, Charge, by many voices, I reiterated it, looking around for my company, but the novelty of the movement by which they were brought into line every company and corps was hopelessly mixed up and confused and there were but few of it with us."[20]

Pvt. Robert P. "Bob" O'Bryan, Co. E., 11th Bn. Tex. Vols., circa 1895. (Lake Charles Daily Press)

O'Bryan went on to describe in detail the horror of the charge on the sugar house and close combat. "Seeing that Texans were in line in the ditch, however, and being intensely excited, I arose out of the ditch, drew my pistol and fired at the sugar house (where I thought I had seen the enemy) almost unconsciously, and crying Charge, Charge, moved forward through the cane and music of flying bullets to another ditch, and continuing forward about 100 yards further emerged into an open potato patch, saw Bob,[21] Dal,[22] and others of the company with me and darted on, making for the sugar house. Saw several men fall in the potato patch while crossing it, but had only one thought which was to arrive with those who were going in that direction, at the sugar house and dislodge the enemy there, and then whatever next presented itself, being entirely ignorant of the enemy's position. Arrive at the sugar house, I with about 15 others got behind a wall (I think)

---

[20] O'Brien Journal, 237.
[21] Robert Perry O'Bryan, 1844-1899, and John Kindallis Bryan, cousins of Capt. O'Bryan.
[22] Charles D. Dodd.

attached some way to the furnace and ran to the other end to an opening on the side next to the enemy. Saw a Yank making from the cabin near there toward the breastwork, levelled my pistol at him, took good aim and fired simultaneously with others.

"The smoke obscured my sight of him and did not know whether he was hurt or not. Got a cap fast in the cylinder of my revolver and could not get it out for sometime, after shooting again and snapping all the other caps got another cap fast and could fire no more during the battle. Before leaving the sugar house heard someone say 'They are in the cabins,' and heard Col. Spaight call for the Batn. I called for Co. E, returned my pistol, drew my sword, and still calling for Co. E, in a storm of bullets, I went with Col. Spaight to the corner of the fence surrounding the negro cabins, saw him and others tear down the fence and perhaps assisted, went on followed by Sam McKee, Harry Potter, Bob O'Bryan, Dal Bryan, Elair Andrus, Benton Spell and others of the Company, to a brick house building within 50 yards of the enemy's breastworks, which I now just discovered they had. Sam McKee was killed behind this house, I saw him die. I remained there sometime in company with Maj. Irvine and at times with Lt. [John B.] Jones, A.A.A. Genl.[23] and others."[24]

Lt. Col. James E. Harrison, acting cmdr. Of Speight's Brigade. (Library of Congress)

Jones then told O'Bryan it would be futile to try to take the breastworks by a frontal assault with the number of men they had. They then retired to a wooden house where they found Colonel Harrison, who ordered them to stop some men retiring to the cane field and with them make a demonstration against the enemy left. O'Bryan, and men with him from his company, went to the levee where he encountered an enemy soldier who wanted to surrender. He wrote, "Calling on the men who were behind and informing them of the fact, we charged up the levee and over it, finding the Yank drawn down in the burs endeavoring to conceal himself but finding that he had been discovered he threw up his hands very pitifully, saying he was wounded, and begged for his life. Ordering him to remain there and calling for the men to fire upon the

---

[23] Lt. John B. Jones became a famous Texas Ranger after the war.
[24] O'Brien Journal, 237-238.

Yankees who were retreating down the levee and to the woods, and after they had fired to follow me, I ran down along the levee to the left, on the enemy's side of it toward and past a position of their battery, I think with my sword drawn and calling on the men to follow—saw a flag approaching over the levee and mistaking it for ours and supposing that Green's dismounted cavalry had come up on our left, I shouted to the men the Victory was ours, yonder is the flag, etc. and continued looking back at the men to advance. Turning to look at the flag again I discovered that I had been mistaken and that it was the enemy's supported by a large fore, about 150 Yanks being in sight. Notifying the men of my error and warning them to retire again to the other side of the levee, and when up on it took another look at them and saw several of my men fire upon them with effect.

"I heard a cry and saw a commotion among them as if someone was wounded, heard a clamoring among them like charge, forward, fire, etc., and seeing their entire line come to the position of aim, I jumped down the other side of the levee, just as the bullets whistled over the levee trimming the weeds and grass on the top of it and throwing them in every direction. I think this volley of the enemy wounded Sol West in the thigh seriously. I had remained behind the levee but a moment when I saw Lt. Jones coming down the levee with his hand to his side, puffing or blowing as if very weak from some cause. I asked him if he was wounded? He answered No, but that he was totally exhausted. He told me to remain with the men while he went to get more. I did not observe him anymore but went up the levee and saw the enemy still advancing and saw them taking position in the yard to fire upon us—looking around I saw only two or three men with me and retired very hastily further to the right where there was a ditch running at a right angle to the levee."[25]

YANKEE'S TRAPPED

Lt. Col. J.B. Leake (Copy print)

Colonel Leake's worst fears had become reality, but he and his men put up as strong a defense as they could. He placed the 19th Iowa to the left of the Sugar Mill and the 26th Indiana to the right. "The rebels knew our exact force, and would they have crossed the Atchafalaya with eight thousand men, cavalry and batteries, on a small steam ferry," only to capture five hundred infantry," Private Dungan wrote. He added, "If there was no positive

---

[25] O'Brien Journal, 239-240.

knowledge on the subject we would yet infer that they had some other object, and it was to attack the division, but our stubborn resistance delayed them till they knew the division was prepared for them, and Gen. Green was heard to order his Adjutant General to order the troops back at once, for they must recross the Atchafalaya that night, for it was too late to go further." Dungan also noted the Federal cavalry and paid an off-hand compliment to Major Boone, saying that if they had made as daring a charge at that Confederal cavalryman, they could have broken the enemy line."[26]

Major John Bruce of the 19th Iowa, who was not present during the battle, filed a report. He said the enemy had turned the Federal right and attacked their rear and cut off retreat. "My regiment was first called into action, met the enemy boldly, and, at short range, delivered a deadly volley, which compelled him [Leake] to fall back. He, however, rallied again in overwhelming force, and, and after a firm and desperate struggle, in which we were well supported by the Twenty-sixth Indiana, we were completely overpowered and compelled to surrender; many of our men, however, refusing to give up until the guns were taken from their hands by the rebels. . . My regiment had only about 260 men in the action, many having been left sick in convalescent camps at Carrollton, La. They were not on the expedition." Bruce also noted that many of the Yankees managed to escape and straggle back to Morganza. He noted, "Great credit is due to the officers and men of my regiment, who fought bravely and desperately against fearful odds. The rebel officers acknowledged it was to them a dearly bought victory, and were much chagrined at finding so small a capture after so vigorous a resistance."[27]

CONFEDERATE *COUP DE GRÂCE*

General Green noted in his report that Boone's and Rountree's battalions delivered the *coup de grâce* on the Federals when he ordered them to attack the bluecoats at Mrs. Stirling's house. But in doing so Boone suffered his two grievous wounds, as Dungan wrote in his history of the battle. But the end was not cut and dried for the gray clad infantry. The "fog of war" was still hanging over the confused battlefield. Captain O'Bryan asked some Confederates in a ditch what they were doing there. "Bob [O'Bryan] came up, one of the men told me I had better get down low in the ditch or I would get shot. I answered that the enemy was coming up the levee to the end of the ditch when their position would be a very

---

[26] Dungan, 90.
[27] O.R., Vol. 26, Pt. 1, 325, 326.

dangerous one, and was begging them to go with me to the levee and stop them. About this time Bob called my attention to the other end of the ditch near the turning row, where I saw our men breaking from the ditch down toward us. This is the only time that I thought of being whipped, and the conclusion was instantly and very painfully forced upon me that if the men could not be stopped and brought back that would inevitably be the result. I started with Bob after them and others who were with us in the ditch followed toward the turning row. I was at the time entirely unconscious of the enemy's bullets, only hearing others say afterwards that we were being heavily fired upon as we retired.

"Arriving at the crowd, or when it had rallied, I saw Col. Spaight talking to his men who were of all the various corps of the Brigade. I asked Col. Spaight, without knowing what he had been saying, what he desired doing, and if they were retiring? He answered not, we must charge. I told him the enemy was whipped and I thought were retreating and told him that I had seen them breaking off to the woods from the levee to our right. He immediately started to the woods from the levee on our right, calling on the men to follow. I, Desire Hargrave, Bob and others of my company, and perhaps 25 others, followed. Seeing men on the breastworks I asked whether it was our men or the enemy. We halted and I discovered that they were shooting at objects on the other side of the levee. Col. Spaight, however, concluded it was the enemy and gave the order to fire upon them, but I stepped up with one or two others and said for God's sake don't fire until it was ascertained positively that it is the enemy, and called the Col's attention to the fact that they were then shooting nearby from us. It was at once concluded that they were our men and the enemy were flying when we moved forward and, reinforced now, to and across the levee, in time to see the Yankees flying in every direction and the victory won." Apparently these were the bluecoats that Boone and Rountree had routed.[28]

O'Bryan said that Mouton's Brigade, except for Clack's 12th Louisiana Battalion, and Semmes' Battery both came up on his part of the field just as the battle ended. Captain Arthur W. Hyatt of the 12th Louisiana noted in his diary that the attack on the Sugar House occurred about 1 o'clock that afternoon. "Making a vigorous attack we drove them from cabin to cabin and finally forced them to take refuge behind the levee. Here they poured in a fire sufficiently destructive to make us much less impetuous than we had been at the commencement. The gallant Major Boon [sic] however coming up at this moment on the Federal flank gave a finishing touch to the fight by a general charge."[29]

---

[28] O'Brien Journal, 241.

[29] Ibid, 242. Bartlett, Napier, *Military Record of Louisiana: Including Biographical and Historical Papers Relating to the Military Organizations of the*

Commissioned officers of the 19th Iowa at the end of the war after they were released from captivity. (Library of Congress)

O'Bryan listed the casualties of his company as Sam McKee and John A. Willis killed: John Andrew McFaddin, missing; Solomon West wounded in the thigh seriously; Robert Burrell and James A. Haney, leg wounds; Jacob Beaumont and Levi McClure, arm wounds. He noted that Lieutenant Ambrose D. Kent went past the brick house where he stepped further to the left behind one of the cabins, where he remained with Sergeant Benton Spell and others. Lieutenant James M Long went around the end of the sugar house and advanced with a number of Company E men to a wood pile and then to the negro cabins.[30]

While the Federals said they were overwhelmed by 5,000 Confederates, General Green said that Speight's Brigade had about 600 men in the fight. He estimated the number of mounted cavalry in the actual fighting, both Boone's and Rountree's battalions, had around 200 men. So, it would appear that both sides had about the same numbers in the actual fight.

The official casualty count for the Federals was a total of 515, including 16 killed, 45 wounded, and 454 captured. That included 237 for the 26th Indiana; 243 for the 19th Iowa; one from the 20th Iowa, Lieutenant Colonel Leake, who was captured; four for the 2nd Illinois Cavalry; five

---

State (Louisiana State University, Baton Rouge and London, paperback edition 1996) 11.
[30] O'Brien Journal, 242.

from the 6th Missouri Cavalry and 25 from the 1st Missouri Light Artillery, Battery E. Those casualties included Lieutenants Silas Kent and John W. Roberts of the 19th Iowa, killed; and Captain Andrew M. Taylor of the 19th Iowa, mortally wounded.[31]

The total Confederate casualties were given as 121, including 26 killed, 85 wounded and 10 men missing. That breaks down per unit to 104 for Speight's Brigade; 12 for Mouton's Brigade (11 for the 12th/16th Louisiana and one in Gray's 28th Louisiana); just two in Boone's (Waller's) Battalion, but including Major Boone; and four in Rountree's Battalion. Green commented in his report that, "The heavy loss sustained by Speight's

Non-commissioned officers of the 19th Iowa at the end of the war after being released from captivity. (Library of Congress)

brigade shows the desperate nature of the conflict, and it is not out of place to mention here, even where all distinguished themselves, the gallant bearing and activity of Lieutenant [John B.] Jones, assistant adjutant-general of Speight's brigade." Green also noted, besides the prisoners, they captured two 10-pounder Parrott guns, with caissons complete, two new ambulances and one hospital wagon, new, filled with medical stores, and two stand of regimental colors belonging to the 19th Iowa and 26th Indiana. There were many small arms and accoutrements captured, and, he added, ". . . every man with an inferior weapon was supplied with a good and efficient one."

---

[31] O.R., Vol. 26, Pt. 1, 325.

The End of the Beginning

The end of the Battle of Stirling's Plantation was just the beginning of that very bloody Fall Campaign that stretched from there, 52 miles south to New Iberia. The campaign also went to Opelousas and then as far west as Chretien Point Plantation, near modern day Sunset, Louisiana. General Green commended his men, saying, "I cannot award too much praise to the troops under my command for their rapid movements under the discouraging effects of a heavy rain and roads knee-deep in mud, and their willingness and enthusiasm to attack the enemy." He also commended by name the top commanders, including Colonel Henry Gray; lieutenant colonels Harrison, Speight,[32] and Clack; and majors Boone and Rountree. He eloquently added in his conclusion, "The gallant dead have proven their devotion to our cause, and the wounded in their silent sufferings have shown that fortitude which a good cause alone could have imbued them with. Notwithstanding the severe march, the troops are ready and anxious to again meet the invader upon our soil."[33]

Green's superior officers, general Mouton and Taylor, in turn praised Green and others. Taylor wrote, "The conduct of Lieutenant-Colonel [J.E.] Harrison, commanding Speight's brigade, and the gallant Major [H.H.] Boone, severely wounded in the engagement, is especially deserving of mention. The recognition of Major Boone, severely wounded in the engagement, is especially deserving of mention. The recognition of Major Boone's gallantry by the Government would be of service to the troops. General Green has fully met the expectations formed from his previous services." Mouton wrote, "To Brigadier-General Green and the officers and men under his command too much praise cannot be awarded."[34]

Although their troops had been defeated, the Northern commanders also commended their men for putting up a good fight under what they thought were overwhelming odds. General Dana wrote, "Of one thing I feel sure—that, after being surprised, they fought as officers and men gallantly, and even after all hope was gone they broke into squads, and endeavored singly to make their escape, in which many succeeded. They sustained the high reputation of veteran soldiers." Major Bruce of the 19th Iowa, wrote, "Great credit is due to the officers and men of my regiment, who fought bravely and desperately against fearful odds. The rebel officers acknowledged it was to them a dearly bought victory, and were chagrined at

---

[32] Unfortunately, Green misspelled Spaight's last name Speight, the colonel of Speight's Brigade, but who was absent. The brigade was led by Harrison.
[33] O.R., Vol. 26, Pt. 1, 331, 332.
[34] Ibid, 329.

finding so small a capture after so vigorous a resistance."

When Dana heard of the debacle at Stirling's Plantation, he agreed to a temporary truce for each side to remove its wounded. "The night of the 29th and the day of the 30th were spent in bringing in our dead and wounded. At daylight yesterday morning [October 1] I sent out the cavalry force, supported by the Thirty-seventh Illinois Volunteer Infantry, all under command of Colonel Black, of that regiment, with orders to push a reconnaissance as much beyond the battle-field as prudence would allow, to push back the pickets of the enemy, to gather whatever information he could, and to make efforts to capture some prisoners, and bring in any public property which the enemy might have been unable to carry off. . . Nineteen rebels badly wounded were found in a building near the field."[35]

On the Confederate side, General Green said after the battle he sent Mouton's Brigade, under Colonel Gray, and the 3rd Cavalry Regiment, Arizona Brigade, to repulse and check the Federals coming down from Morganza. He then went about getting the rest of the command back on the west side of the Atchafalaya. Because of the steepness of the river bank, he could use only one of his flatboats. But he obtained a small steamboat that speeded up the process. "Many of the infantry and dismounted men fell by the roadside, completely exhausted; but all were safely crossed the morning of the 30th," he wrote.[36]

With the fighting winding down there, to the south around New Iberia it was heating up with Banks pushing the 19th and 13th Army Corps up from Brashear City.

---

[35] Ibid, 324.
[36] Ibid, 331.

3 Clashes in Acadiana

Captain Bailie P. L. Vinson, an advance scout or spy, with the 2nd Louisiana Cavalry, had been keeping a close eye on the Federal Army buildup at Brashear City, Louisiana, modern day Morgan city, since October 1, 1863. He sent a remarkably detailed report on the size and strength of the Yankee forces. Vinson was the perfect man for such a daring-do assignment. He was the type of soldier that every nation needs in time of war. A smart and fearless warrior, Vinson, 25 at the time, began the war as a private in the 1st Battalion (Rightor's) Louisiana Infantry in Northern Virginia. Discharged on a certificate of disability August 16, 1861, he was then commissioned a second lieutenant in the 11th Louisiana Infantry November 28, 1861. He fought at the Battle of Shiloh, Tennessee, April 6 and 7, 1862, and the Battle of Farmington, Mississippi May 9, 1862, where he was commended by his division commander. He then resigned June 4, 1862. Vinson returned to Louisiana and was given a captain's commission in the Provisional Army of the Confederate States of America, by Major General Richard Taylor, and was assigned to duty as a scout, which was a euphemism in the war for a spy. Taylor was the commander of the Army of Western Louisiana at the time.[37]

Vinson sent his report back through channels to Major General John

---

[37] O.R., Vol. 26, Pt. 2, P. 340. Confederate Military Service Records, 11th Louisiana Infantry Regiment, Compiled Service Records of Confederate Soldiers Who Served in Organizations from the State of Louisiana. War Records Group 109. National Archives and Records Administration (NARA)M378, Roll 30.

Bankhead Magruder, commander of the Department of Texas. He wrote, "I have just returned from Franklin [Louisiana] from a scout. I send you a correct report of Yankee forces passed through Franklin from the 1st to 15th instant. This report is correct. There is great dissatisfaction among the [enemy] troops, and a great many wish to desert, thinking Texas is a hard road to travel. I brought a Yankee out of their lines, but I am compelled to deliver him, to send him to General Taylor." Vinson reported seeing 26, 12-pounder brass smooth bore guns; 18, 3-inch rifled guns; 4, 30-pounder rifled siege guns; 3, 20-pounder rifled siege guns for a total of 51 artillery pieces. Vinson also counted 1,500 Yankee cavalry; 280 mounted infantry and a total of 20,000 men." The report shows that Vinson was actually behind enemy lines gathering his information and even persuaded one Yankee to desert.[38] The report was then forwarded to General Alfred Mouton, commander of the sub-district of Southwestern Louisiana. He reported that one of his units ambushed the Federal advance cavalry on October 4. The blue coat horse soldiers advanced from Bisland on October 3, and the next day Colonel William G. Vincent's 2nd Louisiana Cavalry temporarily checked the invaders in a skirmish at Nelson's Bridge, about two miles south of New Iberia, Louisiana. The distance between Brashear City and New Iberia along Bayou Teche is about 43 miles. Vincent, commanding 250 troopers in the 2nd Louisiana set up his ambush in a cypress forest along the bayou, and opened up on the Yankee troopers when they crossed a small bridge over a drainage ditch on the S.O. Nelson plantation, known as Nelson's Bridge. The Confederates apparently didn't stick around long enough to count the enemy dead and wounded, but told Mouton the road was filled with bodies. The 2nd Massachusetts Light Artillery (Nim's Battery), quickly came up and opened fire on them. Vincent's men quickly left and reportedly left behind several wounded. Mouton noted a prisoner was also taken and under questioning, told the Confederates the Federals were well equipped with heavy artillery, and he heard the Northerners had as many as 75,000 men, which was clearly an exaggeration, and that they were headed for Texas. "The prisoner is an American, rather intelligent, and

Brig. Gen. Alfred Mouton
SW Dist. Commander
(Photo Hist. of the CW)

---

[38] *OR*, Vol. 26, Pt. 2, 340.

gave the names and numbers of the cavalry regiments, and was made to repeat them, so as to see whether he was telling the truth. His statement was consistent in every instance," Mouton said..[39]

Mouton also said he had pulled the 2nd Louisiana beyond the Vermilion River and left only enough men in front of the advancing Federals to keep an eye on their flanks. He was also waiting on Colonel James P. Major's Texas cavalry brigade to join him to resist the invaders.

General Taylor was getting other reports as well at his headquarters in Alexandria, located in central Louisiana. He was still trying to decide if the Federals were going to move up the Red River to Northwest Louisiana before crossing into Texas, or if they were going to go across the Acadian prairie of Southwest Louisiana via Vermilionville (modern day Lafayette), Lake Charles and Niblett's Bluff on the border with Texas. Niblett's Bluff was a major supply depot and the Confederates were also keeping some 480 prisoners of war there.[40]

Confederate cavalryman
(CDV, author's collection)

Taylor was still puzzling over the exact intentions of the enemy as late as October 11, when he wrote to General Magruder in Texas: "The priest from Abbeville to-day reports that he met on the 10th, on the road from New Iberia to Abbeville, a force of some 2,000 mounted men, escorting a pontoon train. If this be the case, the enemy are going by the Coast road to Niblett's Bluff, crossing the Vermillion and Mermenton [Mermentau] at the lower ferries, and using these streams and the Calcasieu [River], or even this side of that stream, you cannot only materially delay the enemy's movements, but might very likely capture a fleet of supplies or destroy a pontoon train. Such a force could always fall back on Niblett's Bluff as its base." Then on October 20, he wrote to

---

[39] David C. Edmonds, *Yankee Autumn in Acadiana: The Great Texas Overland Expedition* (The Acadiana Press, Lafayette, La. 1979) 44. *OR*, Vol. 26, Pt. 1, 393.
[40] O.R., Vol. 296, Pt. 2, 291.

General Magruder the enemy was skirmishing with General Green around Washington, Louisiana. "A scouting party returned on yesterday from between New Iberia and Abbeville. . . . They report all quiet on the Texas roads; no evidence of a movement in that direction; also that Banks had reached New Iberia, and that the enemy's whole army was in my immediate front. . . I think every preparation should be made to obstruct the river above." The Yankees clearly weren't going to Texas via the coastal route.[41]

By then Banks had already decided the overland route was impracticable. He noted, ". . . I decided, as the only alternative left me for the execution of the orders of the Government, to attempt the occupation of the Rio Grande, which I had suggested on the 13th September as an alternative if the land route was found impracticable. Leaving the troops opposite Berwick Bay upon the land route into Texas, I organized a small expedition, the troops being placed under command of Maj. Gen. N.J.T. Dana, and sailed on the 26th of October, 1863, for the Rio Grande." But there was still plenty of fighting do in Southwest Louisiana before the Fall Campaign would be over.[42]

At the beginning of their campaign, the Federals repeated their practice of looting, pillaging and plundering their way across South Louisiana. They had done the same thing in their Spring Teche Campaign.

BUMMERS AND THIEVES

The military leadership of the Federals, all too often, encouraged lawless and undisciplined behavior, or just ignored it. Fortunately for the historical record, Louisiana Governor Henry Watkins Allen documented the rampage with an investigation compiled as *Official Report Relative to the Conduct of Federal Troops in Western Louisiana During the Invasions of 1863 and 1864*. Many of the allegations in the report are corroborated by reports in the *War of the Rebellion: Official Records of the Union and Confederate Armies*, and unit histories of some of the regiments involved. "Bummers" is a term most often used to describe the Federal soldiers in Major General William Tecumseh Sherman's "March to the Sea" in 1864 in Georgia. Sherman's bummers became infamous for cutting a swath of destruction in Georgia, 60-miles wide, from Atlanta to Savannah on the Atlantic coast. The Federals destroyed homes, barns, slaughtered livestock, killed civilians, abused newly freed slaves, and generally terrorized the population. The exact same behavior was visited on the innocent civilians of Louisiana from the southeastern to northwestern part of the state. Evidence shows that it

---

[41] O.R., Vol. 26, Pt. 1, 387, 388.
[42] Ibid, 19, 20.

wasn't just Sherman's men, loaned to Banks, but also the eastern troops from the North who were equally destructive.[43]

The criminal behavior of the invaders was a reflection of the muddled and corrupt mission given to them by Lincoln. Here are some examples from the report.:

1. The Federalists not only robbed the planters of the produce of their fields, and plundered the goods of merchants; but they destroyed the libraries and depositories of professional men.
2. They sacked private dwellings, and while reveling upon the contents of the pantries and wine cellars, they grossly and indecently insulted the unprotected females, and wantonly destroyed their last remnants of food and clothing. They shattered the crockery, glass-ware, and mirrors, strewing the floor with their fragments; they stove, with the butts of their muskets, the doors of side-boards and closets, pried open drawers with the points of their bayonets, and slashed with their sabres prized objects of taste, or ornaments consecrated to pious uses; when their intoxication, or the excitement of a general license has subsided, they dashed to pieces and burned for fuel costly articles of furniture, and prized heir-looms from former generals.
3. They violently plundered the rich of their money, the poor of their necessary effects, the women of their jewelry, and even the children of their trinkets. Nor did they spare the dead. They sacrilegiously

Gov. Henry Watkins Allen
(Library of Congress)

---

[43] Governor Henry Watkins Allen, edited and annotated by David C. Edmonds, *The Conduct of Federal Troops in Louisiana During the Invasions of 1863 and 1864* (The Acadian Press, Lafayette, La. 1988) 3-11.

ravished from them the last covering which enclosed their mortal remains.
4. They fired volleys among private citizens, and groups of women and children, in the streets of a peaceful village.
5. They violated the sanctuary of the tomb.
6. They arbitrarily arrested peaceful and unoffending citizens, whom they dragged through the country like felons; whom they confined under guard in exposed situations, or lodged in jails from which they had loosed the depraved and criminals; or, whom they transported to a distant city, to languish for months in prison, a prey to the cares and anxieties haunting the victim thus rudely torn from his family.
7. In violation of the decencies and proprieties of life, they unnecessarily occupied private dwellings, or surrounded them with their camps, so that helpless ladies were driven to seek refuge in interior rooms, where, besides the annoyances of interrupted privacy, and the apprehension of more serious intrusion, they were deprived of the comforts, and, sometimes, of the necessaries of life.
8. They not only razed to their foundations, or wantonly burned plantation buildings and dwellings, from which they had driven the inmates; but they tore down, over their heads, the sheltering roof of the widow and the orphan.
9. They destroyed not only poultry, the flocks and herds, the fields, the gardens, and the orchards, and attempted to destroy the sources of salt, all essential to sustain and preserve life, but they also destroyed the medicines and surgical instruments, indispensable to restore health. They not only chopped to pieces or burned the aratory instruments, the carts and wagons, the corn and sugar mills necessary for the production of new supply of food; but they hacked to pieces the cards, the spinning wheels, and the looms required to furnish the necessary clothing; and, as if this were not sufficient to gratify the most refined malignity, they introduced loathsome diseases among the people whom they had previously despoiled.
10. While thus violating on the one hand the law of the Christian, and, on the other, the precept of the Mohammedan, they set at naught both, by neither keeping faith nor covenant with those they drove to accept their protection, on the condition of professed allegiance, nor with the credulous Negroes, whom they had perfidiously drawn to their toils. [44]

---

[44] Allen-Edmonds, 15-18.

CONFEDERATES GATHER

General Taylor didn't have time to celebrate the victory at Stirling's Plantation. By October 1 it was already obvious that another major invasion of his home state was underway. He wrote on October 6, "There is no doubt that the enemy is advancing in very large force." Taylor also rode out from his headquarters in Alexandria himself to survey the situation first hand. He began gathering his forces for resistance to the invasion, although he knew they were heavily outnumbered. Captain O'Bryan of Spaight's Battalion noted in his diary on October 4 at Morgan's Ferry that they had been ordered the next day to start a westward movement. He speculated, "It is said our destination is Belle Cheney Springs." The next day, Monday, October 5, the gray clad infantry marched 14 miles. The next day they continued the westward march and arrived three miles above Washington, Louisiana, which is near Opelousas, and a landing on Bayou Courtableau, which feeds into Bayou Teche. Then on October 7 they were diverted northward toward Alexandria.[45]

Brig. Gen. Thomas Green
(Confederate Veteran Magazine)

---

[45] O'Bryan's Journal, 414.

Mouton's Brigade returned to Camp at Morgan's Ferry the evening after the battle, and on October 1 took up another march that led them through Bayou de Glaize, Simmesport, Bayou Rouge, Bayou Cane, Evergreen, and finally linked up with Walker's Texas Infantry on October 5 at Moreauville. One of the Texans, who was born in Ireland, Private Joseph P. Blessington, recorded his impression of the Louisianians in his diary. He wrote, "Marched eighteen miles; passed through the village of Moreauville. At this place we met Mouton's Division of Louisiana troops, who were nearly all dressed in Federal uniforms that they had captured at Brashear City. They were a fine body of troops, and did good service in the Attakapas country." By this time the Great Texas Overland Expedition was well underway.[46]

General Franklin, with his segment of the 19th Army Corps, had moved slowly toward Bayou Teche. The 2nd Louisiana Cavalry and Major's Texas Cavalry Brigade had skirmished with advance elements of the enemy October 9 at Vermilionville at the bridge over the bayou. It was an uneven match with the Confederates, who numbered less than a 1,000 men against two Federal divisions and three batteries of crack artillery. The Texans and Louisianians withdrew after a brief exchange of fire. Meanwhile the heavy Texas and Louisiana infantry were up in the vicinity of Washington, Louisiana between Opelousas and Alexandria.[47]

THE BATTLE OF BUZZARD'S PRAIRIE

By mid-October the slow-moving Federals were facing increasing Southern resistance. They established a camp at Bayou Carion Crow [or Carencro or Buzzard's Prairie] on October 11 between Vermilionville and Opelousas. Franklin reported, "My advance arrived here about 11 a.m., the enemy falling back before them. There is no doubt that the rebel Generals Mouton, Major, and Green passed here yesterday, bound north. Their object must have been to get information from their spies, or to select a place to fight. They left this house early this morning. Yesterday five or six guns (bronze) passed north; two of them were left here to defend the passage of the bayou, but they were taken away this morning. We fired eight shots, and the force that was here immediately left."[48]

---

[46] Bartlett, Pt. 3, 11. Joseph P. Blessington, Campaigns of Walker's Texas Division (State House Press, Austin, Texas 1994) 135.
[47] Winters, 298. Edmonds, 85. Blessington, 135. Alwyn Barr, *Polignac's Texas Brigade,* (Texas A&M University Press, College State, Texas, 1998) 129.
[48] O.R., Vol. 26, Pt. 2; 337.

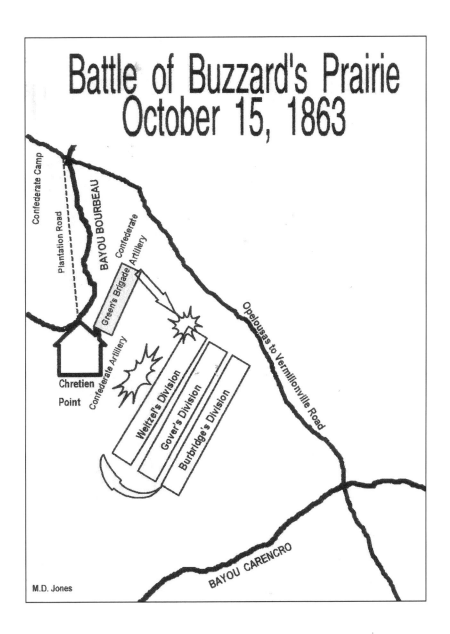

Over the next few days, Franklin put out scouts to find the enemy and he got a report from Brigadier General Godfrey Weitzel, commanding the 1st Division of the 19th Army Corps, reported that the Confederates has some 10,000 men before them, which was a good estimate. On October 14, Bank's detached Colonel Edmund Davis' Cavalry Brigade. Franklin responded he had enough infantry but needed more cavalry. Things really began heating up for the Yankees the night of the 14th. Franklin had Weitzel's Division, and Brigadier General Cuvier Grover's 3rd Division, both of the 19th Army Corps; and Brigadier General Stephen Burbridge's Division of the 13th Army Corps, on hand. Confederate General Green brought up his artillery, and as soon as "Taps" was sounded in the Federal camps, the rebel long-range 10-pounder Parrot guns opened up a nightlong bombardment with little damage done, but the bluecoats were kept awake and on edge.[49]

Maj. Gen. Willam B. Franklin
(Library of Congress)

General Green, who was commanding a division of cavalry, had on immediate hand his own brigade, being commanded by Colonel William P. "Gotch" Hardeman of the 4th Texas Cavalry. The brigade was made up of the 4th, 5th and 7th cavalry regiments, and the Valverde Battery of Captain Joseph Sayers, on the Confederate left flank and Captain Oliver Semmes' 1st Confederate Battery, on the right. On the morning of the 15th, Green had the cavalry dismounted and lined up behind a fence on Mrs. Chretien's Plantation. Hardeman "opened the ball" at daylight and led out three companies, one from each regiment, to skirmish with the Federals. Franklin countered by ordering Weitzel's Division, made up of two brigades, which, when lined up in line of battle, stretched for a mile, to move forward against the Confederates. Behind them were the divisions of Grover and Burbridge. They also had an overwhelming superiority in artillery. The outnumbered Confederates were steadily driven back. The Southern artillery, however, then opened fire and all three Texas cavalry regiments charged the Federal right.[50]

---

[49] Edmonds, 164. O.R., Vol. 26, Pt. 2, 338.
[50] Edmonds, 164 165.

Col. William Hardeman
(Copy print)

The stunned bluecoat infantry temporarily folded, but then, at 7 o'clock, a section of Captain Ormond Nims' 1st Massachusetts Battery blasted the Texans with grape and canister, repulsing the attackers. Then another section of the Massachusetts gunners opened fire on Semmes' Confederate Battery, exploding an ammunition chest and killing two Confederate artillerymen. . .The *Houston Tri-Weekly Telegraph* newspaper reported that seven men in the all German Company G, 4th Texas, were killed by the enemy artillery in one explosion. The fighting continued and at 10 o'clock, Burbridge's Division arrived on the field from Vermilionville with heavy reinforcements of artillery. A Wisconsin soldier with Burbridge, wrote that their eastern compatriots in the 19th Army Corps cheered the westerners as they marched around their left flank and into the attack on the Confederates. He wrote that they "thought they had bushed a grizzley and daresent fotch him so they sent for the western boys."

An Ohio soldier with the 96th volunteers, who was with Burbridge, wrote, "On the 15th we heard the artillery of the rebels, and prepared to march immediately to the support of the Nineteenth Corps, encamped on Carrion Crow Bayou. The artillery duel which followed resulted in the repulse of the enemy. The 1st Brigade of the Thirteenth Army Corps now came up, passing the Nineteenth in camp, and advanced to Bayou Borbeau, where it halted soon after. On the 21st we were again on the march, and, meeting the enemy, were surprised that, after the loss of a few killed, wounded an prisoners, they should fall back from so strong a position and permit us to press, without further trouble, to Barnes' Landing."[51]

Seeing that they were hopelessly out-numbered and out-gunned, Hardeman ordered a retreat, but not before setting up a deadly ambush. He placed the 7th Texas, dismounted, at a coulee, which crossed the Chretien plantation road, while the 4th and 5th Texas skirmished with oncoming Federals. After the bluecoats crossed Bayou Bourbeau, they were completely surprised when the hidden Texans opened fire on them, adding to the attackers' casualty total.[52]

---

[51] J.T. Woods, M.D., *Services of the Ninety-sixth Ohio Volunteers* (Blade Printing and Paper Co., Toledo, Ohio 1874) 39.
[52] Edmonds, 165.

General Taylor arrived three days after the fight at Bayou Bourbeau, October 18, and took personal command of the infantry. The infantry still had not been used, but Green's cavalry continued to do most of the skirmishing with the slow moving enemy. In fact, Banks had already determined to call off the overland expedition due to the difficulty of supplying such a large army over the long stretch of sparsely settled prairies between Vermilionville and Niblett's Bluff. Banks dispatched another amphibious expedition toward Texas. The second division of the 13th Army Corps was dispatched October 26 to plant the flag on the soil of the Lone Star State near the border with Mexico. With little opposition, the expedition easily occupied Point Isabel and Brownsville. He would soon find out this was a useless victory since neither Washington nor the high command supported it. It was also a desolate area and far away from the population centers of Houston and Galveston. But Banks hoped to keep Confederate forces occupied in South Louisiana while he consolidated his gains. Meanwhile, at the same time October 18, Taylor was strengthening Mouton's infantry command with the Texas infantry brigade of Brigadier General Jules Marie, Prince de Polignac. The French prince could work well with Mouton since both spoke the Gallic language. Polignac's Brigade was formed by combining it with Speight's Brigade, which then consisted of the 15th Texas Infantry, 17th, 22nd and 34th Texas cavalry regiments (dismounted) and temporarily the infantry portion of A. W. Spaight's 11th Texas Battalion.[53]

BATTLE OF OPELOUSAS

The next significant military action took place on October 21, when a sharp skirmish between the Confederate cavalry and the Federals clashed about three miles south of Opelousas. Colonel John Fonda's cavalry brigade and two infantry brigades of the 13th Army Corps led the bluecoats. The first skirmish occurred at the plantation of Charles and Celestine Lavergne, where the 5th Texas Cavalry was on picket duty. When they spotted the Federals coming at them, they mounted up and retreated to Bayou Tesson, where they reported the enemy was on the march. Colonel Fonda had ordered his own 118th Illinois (mounted) Infantry to charge them.[54]

When the Federal infantry arrived, there were 12,000 bluecoats arrayed against Green's gray jackets, 3,000 troopers at the most. Colonel William

---

[53] Winters, 298. Silas T. Grisamore, edited by Arthur W. Bergeron Jr., *Reminiscences of Uncle Silas: A History of the 18th Louisiana Infantry* (Louisiana State University Press, Baton Rouge and London, 129) 129. Barr, 29.
[54] Edmonds, 204.

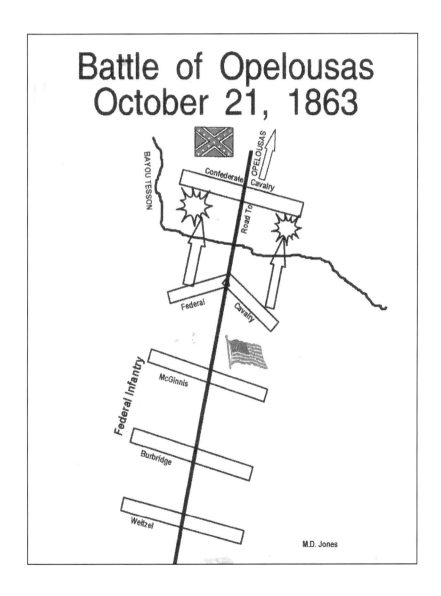

Barney of the 29th Wisconsin Infantry, Brigadier George McGinnis' Division, wrote of the spectacle, "Ours was the first line and composed of five regiments marching by the front with fixed bayonets and colors flying, the whole presented a sight well worth the seeing. When our skirmishers, of which each regiment sent out two companies deployed about six feet apart, commenced firing, our brigade sent up one of those cheers such as Westerners only can give and it was took up by the next line, then by the next of the XIX Corps who cheered as loud as Eastern men can cheer—which is not loud." Barney added, "The rebs at that moment advanced in splendid style—by the rear rank! Such skedaddling no persons can imagine who never saw Secesh run when hard pressed by the Yankee barbarians." But after the invaders got north of Bayou Tesson, the 5th Texas put up a last ditch fight which momentarily halted the Federals, but they soon made an unobstructed move into Opelousas.[55]

Franklin wrote to Banks of the small affair, "The head of my column has arrived here. The enemy made a stand about 3 miles out. They had nine regiments of cavalry, two battalions of infantry, and three or four guns. A little shelling drove them away. I leave at once for Barre's Landing, and shall encamp near there to-night with the infantry. Part of the cavalry will go there to-night." He then reported two days later that any further movements were being delayed by a storm and by the scarcity of forage for the horses and mules. The next day he was able to send out a cavalry patrol that determined the Confederates were in full retreat toward Alexandria. Of the lack of supplies in the area, he wrote, "There is absolutely nothing within reach. General Washburn's force, with the exception of what he left at Vermillion, in obedience to orders received from department headquarters, and that left on the Teche, New Iberia, and Franklin, is now here; also the train, with fifteen days' supplies. . . But there is very little forage in the country, and a move somewhere must soon be made. The forage in the country is important, and I think that we must get nearer to New Iberia or the Mississippi River."[56]

Banks was preoccupied with his landing on the South Texas coast, and Franklin was not getting any direction on what he should do next. He wrote on November 1, 1863, "I have received the two communications from you [Brig. Gen. Charles P. Stone, Banks' chief of staff in New Orleans] and from the commanding general. I have been obliged to return to this place, Carrion Crow Bayou, on account of scarcity of forage and doubt about supplies. The roads are getting exceedingly bad. One of the Objects which you suggest will be attained by building a bridge across the Mementon. As

---

[55] Ibid, 207.
[56] O.R., Vol. 26, Pt. 1, 340, 341.

soon as possible this will be done. Please order the telegraph laid to Vermilion, where I go with the Nineteenth Corps to-morrow, leaving the Thirteenth here. The cavalry will be divided between the post."

Franklin was floundering and also trying to work with the jayhawkers, outlaws led by Ozeme Carriere, as scouts. His band of desperadoes consisted on deserters from both armies as well as conscript evaders who had been robbing and murdering the scattered, isolated farm families on the Acadian prairie. But Franklin found them to be unreliable allies. He wrote, "Ever since the march up the Teche began, I have heard of Jose Cavriere [Ozeme Carriere] and his men. I have sent for him three times, and while our force was at Opelousas he had ample time to come in. But neither he nor any of his men came. Perhaps the fact that the country in that vicinity is infested with small guerrilla bands, and that these people did not believe that we intend to hold the country, may have kept them from coming in, but the fact is patent that none of them came." Franklin's forces had become badly scattered and vulnerable.[57]

Louisiana "scouts" were really jayhawkers (outlaws) who General Franklin found unreliable in enemy territory.
(Library of Congress)

---

[57] Ibid, 342.

4 BATTLE OF BAYOU BOURBEAU

With the Federals floundering, the Confederates were gathering for a strike on the rearguard of the invaders of their country. General Taylor, who was now at the front with his Army of Western Louisiana, had been keeping a close eye on the enemy movements, and waiting for an opportunity to strike. He had tried to engage with his entire army on October 24. Taylor wrote on October 25, "Yesterday morning the enemy advanced 5 miles above Washington, on the Boeuf road. We were drawn up to oppose them or fight; the enemy, however, declined, and returned to Washington [Louisiana]. Last night, Colonel Major captured 23 of the Thirteenth Corps below Opelousas. We have beaten the enemy in a number of skirmishes, taking prisoners. He, however, declines any serious engagement unless he has his whole force in hand. No movement toward the west. All the recent prisoners say the expedition is going to Alexandria and Shreveport. I have moved my forces to the Huffpower [Bayou Hoffpauir], as we have entirely consumed the forage on the Lower Boeuf. In addition, I can throw more cavalry on the prairies to the enemy's left, not having the Big Cane to guard."[58]

When he determined that the Yankees were in retreat, he ordered General Green to follow them and severely harass their rearguard. He reported, "On the 2d [of November], the enemy withdrew from Opelousas,

---

[58] Ibid, 390, 391, 392.

Colonel [J.P.] Major, with his brigade, skirmishing briskly with the enemy all day and delaying his movements Late in the day, General Green pursued him with Green's brigade, commanded by Colonel [A.P.] Bagby, and the three regiments of infantry, with a section of the Valverde Battery, Lieutenant P.G. Hume, and a section of Captain J.M. Daniel's Battery commanded by Lieutenant Samuel Hamilton. General Green made his preparations for attacking the following morning. The enemy's rear guard was encamped on the Bourbeau, 7 miles below Opelousas." The infantry which Taylor referred to was the brigade of Colonel Oran M. Roberts, and included the 11th Texas Infantry Regiment (not the 11th Texas Battalion which had fought at Stirling's Plantation), which was Roberts' own regiment under the command of Lieutenant Colonel James H. Jones; the 15th Texas Infantry under Lieutenant Colonel James E. Harrison, which had fought so well at Stirling's Plantation; and the 18th Texas Infantry commanded by Colonel Wilburn H. King. They would carry the heavy punch in the battle and their Texas brothers in the cavalry would swarm around the Yankee foe to disconcert him. While the 15th Texas was the only one of the three infantry regiments that had experienced combat, all had been in service for over a year and were well trained, hardened by long marches and camp life, and ready to fight.59

Col. Oran Milo Roberts was a pre-war Texas Supreme Court Justice and a post-war Texas governor. (Copy print)

Colonel Roberts was already an important figure in Texas before the war. He was a Justice of the Texas Supreme court and one of the leaders of the secession movement in 1861. He was born July 9, 1815 in Laurens District, South Carolina and home schooled until he was 17-years-old. He received his higher education at the University of Alabama, where he graduated in 1836. Roberts was admitted to the Alabama State Bar in 1837

---

59 Ibid, 391, 392. Blessington, 140.

and then served a term in the Alabama legislature. He immigrated to the independent Republic of Texas in 1841, where he settled in the town of San Augustine to practice law. In 1844, the young lawyer was appointed district attorney by President Sam Houston. Then in 1846, Roberts was appointed a district judge in the new State of Texas by Governor James Pinckney Henderson. He was elected to the Texas Supreme Court in 1856 and became a proponent of states' rights, and then the secession movement. Roberts was unanimously elected president of the Texas Secession Convention January, 1861, which took the Lone Star State out of the Union, over the objections of then Governor Sam Houston. In 1862, he helped organize the 11th Texas Infantry in Houston, in which he then served as colonel.[60]

Col. Arthur P. Bagby Jr.
(Library of Congress)

The leader of Green's Texas Cavalry Brigade was Colonel Arthur Pendleton Bagby Jr. He was born May 17, 1833 in Claiborne, Alabama. His father was an Alabama politician who served his state in the House of Representatives and the U.S. Senate in Washington, D.C. The younger A.P. Bagby attended schools in the capital city and then attended the U.S. Military Academy in West Point, New York, where he graduated at age 19 and became commissioned a second lieutenant. Bagby then served on frontier duty, 1852-53, at Fort Chadbourne, Texas. Bagby resigned his commission to study law and was admitted to the Alabama State Bar in 1855, and practiced in Mobile. In 1858, he moved to Gonzales, Texas and there, married Frances Taylor in June, 1860. Upon the outbreak of war, he raised a company of volunteers in the summer of 1861, which became part of the 7th Texas Cavalry. He served in the regiment as major, lieutenant colonel and then colonel. The regiment was attached to Brigaider General Henry H. Sibley's Army of New Mexico and took part in battles of Valverde and Glorieta Pass. After that campaign, Sibley took part in the Battle of Galveston, serving as "Horse Marines" and

---

[60] Ford Dixon, "ROBERTS, ORAN MILO," *Handbook of Texas Online* (http://www.tshaonline.org/handbook/online/articles/fro18), accessed September 26, 2015.

Capt. Josep D. Sayers
(Library of Congress)

helping to capture the *U.S.S. Harriet Lane*. Moved into Western Louisiana in the spring of 1863 for the first Teche Campaign, Bagby played a particularly important part in the Battle of Bisland Plantation on April 13, 1863, where he was wounded.[61]

CONFEDERATE ARTILLERY

Also playing a key role in the Battle of Bayou Bourbeau was the Valverde Battery. The battery consisted of five guns, three 6-pounders and two 12-pounder howitzers, which had been captured at the Battle of Valverde, New Mexico on February 21, 1862, by Sibley's Texas Brigade. The battery was organized around the captured guns with volunteers from the Texas cavalrymen. Captain Joseph Draper Sayers was given command of the 75-man battery. Sayers was just 20-years-old at the time but had a military education at the Bastrop Military Institute from 1852 to 1860. He started the war in Green's 5th Texas Cavalry where he had served with distinction. Officially organized June 1, 1862 at Fort Bliss, Texas, the battery actually received its baptism of fire earlier on April 15, 1862 at a skirmish at Peralta, New Mexico Territory. In that spring 1863 Teche Campaign, the battery was notable for helping to capture the Federal gunboat, *U.S.S. Diana*, in March of that year. It was also in the Battle of Bisland Plantation April 13, 1863 where Captain Sayers was severely wounded. Sayers was replaced by Captain Timothy D. Nettles, who commanded at the Battle of Bayou Bourbeau and led the Valverde Battery for the rest of the war.[62]

General Taylor was very proud of his Texas troops. Of the men of Green's brigade, he wrote, "The men were hardy and many of the officers brave and zealous, but the value of these qualities was lessened by lack of

---

[61] Craig H. Roell, "BAGBY, ARTHUR PENDLETON," *Handbook of Texas Online*(http://www.tshaonline.org/handbook/online/articles/fba05), accessed September 26, 2015. Uploaded on June 12, 2010. Modified on March 1, 2011.

[62] Donald S. Frazier, "VAL VERDE BATTERY," *Handbook of Texas Online*(http://www.tshaonline.org/handbook/online/articles/qkv01), accessed September 26, 2015. Uploaded on June 15, 2010. Modified on March 8, 2011.

discipline. In this, however, they surpassed most of the mounted men who subsequently joined me, discipline among them 'shining by its utter absence.' Their experience in war was limited to hunting down Comanches and Lipans, and, as in all new societies, distinctions of rank were unknown. Officers and men addressed each other as Tom, Dick, or Harry, and had no more conception of military gradations than of the celestial hierarchy of the poets. I recall an illustrative circumstance. A mounted regiment arrived from Texas, which I rode out to inspect. The profound silence in the camp seemed evidence of good order. The men were assembled under the shade of some trees, seated on the ground, and much absorbed. Drawing near, I found the colonel seated in the center, with a blanket spread before him, on which he was dealing the fascinating game of monte. Learning that I would not join the sport, this worthy officer abandoned his amusement with some displeasure. It was a scene for that illustrious inspector Colonel Martinet to have witnessed."[63]

Private Blessington of the 16th Texas Infantry also reminisced on why Texans of that era made such good soldiers. He wrote, "Texans are born soldiers; from early boyhood they are taught the use of the rifle and six-shooter. They know that much depends on their skill in the use of arms—the safety of themselves and their families from the murdering Lipan, or the ruthless Comanche. They learn in early childhood what has contributed to the fame of the French solider—perfect self-reliance at all times and under all circumstances. This, perhaps, is the most valuable quality a soldier can possess. Without it the most thorough bull-dog courage often ends in a worse sacrifice of life. The Texan possesses another high quality of a soldier—power of endurance, and ability to march when suffering for food and water, that would prostrate men not trained to travel the immense prairies of Texas, where they are often for days without either."[64]

FEDERAL LEADERSHIP

Brigadier General Stephen Gano Burbridge was the main Federal leader in the battle. He commanded the 4th Division of the 13th Army Corps but had on hand only one brigade of infantry and one brigade of cavalry with him at the battle. Burbridge was born August 19, 1831 in Georgetown, Kentucky and attended Georgetown College and the Kentucky Military Institute at Frankfort. He pursued a career as a lawyer but with the outbreak of war became colonel of the 26th Kentucky Infantry (Union). He gained distinction at the Battle of Shiloh and was promoted to brigadier general

---

[63] Taylor, 126.
[64] Blessington, 14, 15.

June 9, 1862. Burbridge was given command of the troops in his native state, and then distinguished himself in the Vicksburg campaign. He was then among the reinforcements for Banks to carry out the Fall Teche Campaign.[65]

Fonda was leading the cavalry with his own 118th Illinois and Lieutenant Colonel Hari Robinson's 1st Louisiana Cavalry (Union), which had been consolidated with the 2nd Rhode Island Cavalry, causing a near mutiny among the Rhode Islanders. The mutinous unit had already accumulated a bad reputation for marauding. Also with the horse soldiers were the 6th Missouri Cavalry, Major Bacon Montgomery; and the 14th New York Cavalry under the command of Lieutenant Colonel John Cropsey. The infantry brigade, commanded by Colonel Richard Owen, consisted of the 60th Indiana, Captain Augustus Goelzer; 67th Indiana, Lieutenant Colonel Theodore Buehler; 83rd Ohio, Colonel Frederick Moore; 96th Ohio, Lieutenant Colonel Albert Brown; and 23rd Wisconsin, Colonel Joshua Guppey. The artillery support consisted of the 17th Ohio Battery, commanded by Captain Charles Rice, and Lieutenant William Marland's section of the 2nd Massachusett's (Nim's) Battery. Burbridge said he had about 1,600 men in all. But there were large reinforcements within a few miles march.[66]

Brig. Gen. Stephen G. Burbridge
(National Archives)

Burbridge reported, "My camp was situated about 3 miles from Bayou Carrion Crow, near the head of a small bayou which runs in the direction of Opelousas through a ravine 1 mile wide. Upon each side was an extensive prairie." Green's cavalry caught up with the Federal rearguard and started pressing them hard on November 2. "After having sufficiently reconnoitered the position of the enemy, I determined to attack him, and made my dispositions accordingly," Green said. "Colonel Roberts, in command of the three regiments of infantry before mentioned, was assign-

---

[65] John E. Kleber, The Kentucky Encyclopedia (The University Press of Kentucky, Lexington, Ky. 1992) 142.
[66] Edmonds, 406, 407.

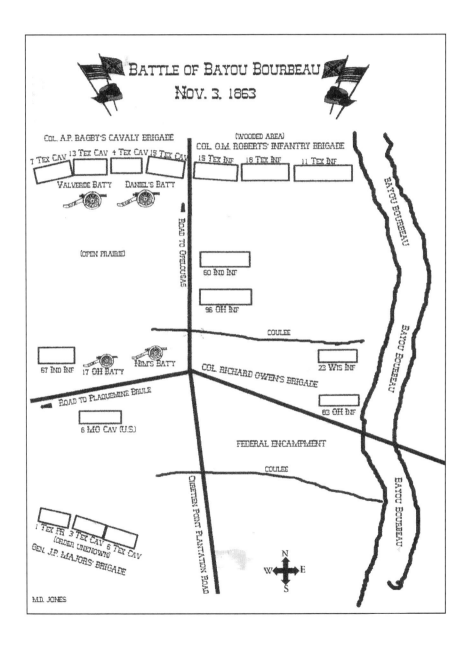

ed to the command of our left wing, and was directed to sweep down the Bellevue road and occupy the timber below the enemy on the bayou, and assail his right flank."[67]

Green then set out his order of battle for the fight. "Colonel [J.P.] Major, with his brigade of cavalry, constituted our right wing, while Colonel [A.P.] Bagby, with his brigade of cavalry, occupied our center. Two of his regiments (the Fourth and Fifth,) were dismounted, and acted as infantry for the occasion, supporting our artillery, which consisted of a rifle section of Daniel's battery and a section of the Valverde, commanded respectively, by Lieutenants [Samuel M.] Hamilton and [P.G.] Hume, both sections being placed for the occasion under the command of Lieutenant Morse. These disposition having been made, and the brigade commanders occupying the ground assigned to them, I ordered an immediate advance."[68]

Burbridge was fully expecting the attack on the morning of November 3. "This conviction was made more sure by 6 of the First Louisiana Cavalry deserting from the reserve pickets Monday night (2d), and going over to the enemy. Early on the morning of the 3d, our outposts were driven in, and a heavy force seen on our front and left. This intelligence was sent to General Washburn promptly; our lines formed, the artillery gotten into place, and a few well-directed rounds from the artillery and some maneuvering soon made him retire. About 10 o'clock a.m. but few of the enemy could be seen. I directed the troops then to retire to camp, but hold themselves ready to fall in at a moment's warning. Sent a dispatch to Major General Washburn that the enemy had nearly all retired out of sight, and, after reconnoitering my left in person, returned to my headquarters."[69]

On the Confederate left, Colonel Roberts reported he had the 15th Texas Infantry, with 275 men, on his right; the 18th Texas, with 320 men in his center; and the 11th Texas, numbering 355 infantrymen, on his left. The total number of his brigade, with support personnel, was 950 men. He added that Captain H.W. Fisher's Company G of the 7th Texas Cavalry was also attached to his command to act as flanking scouts as they approached the Federal line. "These regiments were joined together under my command at Opelousas one hour before daylight on the morning of the 3rd after two days of rapid and fatiguing march down Bayou Boeff [Boeuf]. He coordinated with General Green with a member of Green's staff, Captain J.E. Hart, attached to Roberts for the battle. Also helping Roberts coordinate with the various regiments were Sergeant Major Allen Kirby of the 18th Texas, Sergeant Major Sam H. Coupland and Private F.W. Johnson,

---

[67] O.R., Vol. 26, Pt. 1, 359, 393, 394.
[68] Ibid, 394.
[69] Ibid, 360.

of his own regiment, the 11th Texas, all being mounted.⁷⁰

General Green reported that Roberts' infantry commenced the attack about 11 a.m. by driving in enemy skirmishers: "Our infantry was engaged for half an hour before our cavalry and dismounted troopers, with the artillery, were closely engaged on our right and center. Our infantry was most stubbornly resisted by the enemy, but they gallantly and steadily moved forward, without for a moment faltering, under a most terrific fire of artillery and musketry." Roberts said his skirmishers consisted of Company C of the 11th Texas, and companies A and F of the 15th.

Col. Wilburn H. King
18th Texas Infantry
(Confederate Veteran Magazine)

Since none of the men of the 18th Texas had rifles, they had smoothbore muskets, he did not include any of its companies in the skirmishers, who typically push ahead of the main battle line.

Burbridge had stationed his forces in a somewhat disorderly, spread out fashion. He said, "The rebel infantry approached through a ravine from the direction of Opelousas. Upon the left, across the prairie, a heavy column of cavalry could be seen moving upon me in line of battle. I directed one of my largest regiments, the Sixty-seventh Indiana, about 260 strong, one section of Nims' battery, and one section of the Seventeenth Ohio Battery, to take a position on my left. I then posted about 150 cavalry on their left, and directed the whole to guard against an attack on my rear and left. My remaining three regiments, the Eighty-third Ohio being out guarding foraging trains, and four pieces of artillery (Seventeenth Ohio Battery), I posted so as to meet the rebel infantry in the ravine. The cavalry, under Colonel Fonda, One hundred and eighteenth Illinois, was intrusted with guarding my right." The 23rd Wisconsin Infantry, commanded by Colonel Joshua Guppey, was further to the rear on the Federal right behind

---

⁷⁰ Oran M. Roberts, edited by Alwyn Barr, "The Battle of Bayou Bourbeau, November 3, 1863: Colonel Oran M. Roberts' Report, *Louisiana History: The Journal of the Louisiana Historical Association*, Vol. 6, No. 1 (Winter, 1965) pp. 83-91.

a coulee.[71]

Col. Joshua J. Guppey
23rd Wisconsin Infantry
(Library of Congress)

Colonel Guppey reported they were expecting and early morning attack and were ready when the rebels appeared before them. "The enemy, however, retired from our picket lines, and, after the brigade had been under arms some hours, the men were permitted to stack arms and return to their quarters, but were directed to keep on their equipments and be ready to fall in at a moment's notice. After the alarm had subsided, the Eighty-third Ohio Volunteers, with the wagons of the brigade, were sent out on a foraging expedition," he wrote. Two paymasters also set up for balloting for an election being held in their home state. But this routine was soon interrupted by gunfire.

"The firing from the direction of the Sixtieth Indiana, both musketry and artillery, became very heavy and well sustained, and, in a short time, I saw that our force was falling back. I then learned that the Sixtieth Indiana and the artillery with it had encountered a brigade of infantry, accompanied by artillery and cavalry," Guppey wrote. He added up to that time they had no inkling that Confederate infantry was in their front.[72]

General Green, masterfully coordinating the various elements of his command, said, "Our artillery was brought up within 400 yards of a line of the enemy's infantry, in front of their encampment, and fired a few shots into them, but about this time the cavalry, under Colonel Major, on our extreme right, dashed into the left flank of the enemy, while Colonel Bagby, with Herbert's regiment and Waller's battalion, mounted, and Hardeman's and McNeill's regiments, dismounted, charged them in front, the cavalry making on a partially concealed foe, the most brilliant charge on record. Our gallant infantry, under their brave officers, had given the enemy such a chastisement on his right flank, pushing him back to his encampment, that the whole Federal force gave way as soon as the engagement became general and close."[73]

---

[71] O.R., Vol. 26, Pt. 1, 360.
[72] Ibid, 365.
[73] Ibid, 394.

Corporal Reuben B. Scott of Company A, 67th Indiana Infantry, recounted what it was like being overwhelmed by the rebel assault. He wrote, "Green's whole troop is coming steadily over the prairie, when Gen. Burbrage [sic] sends his aid, Capt. Friedley, to Col. Buhler, ordering him to fall back, which Buhler refuses to do. When Burbrage again sends Friedley, peremptorily ordering Buhler to fall back to the woods. But it is now too late, as Green's masses were upon us with a heavy cavalry force pushing between us and the main army, and entirely surrounding us when our artillery was pouring shot and shell, while the rebel batteries were [also] pouring a heavy fire of shot and shell into us; and now we open our musketry upon the advancing columns, and they pour a storm of Minnie [balls] into our ranks; and by this time the cavalry was charging us, upon flank and rear, and our artillery had fallen back and was pouring into the rebels and us a storm of canister, while the rebel batteries were pouring into us and their men a storm of grape; while at this juncture both forces became all mixed, and a pandemonium of sticking with bayonets, clubbing of muskets and shooting with revolvers. Meanwhile a storm of grape and canister was pouring into this fighting mass both from front and rear, while a cloud of smoke is spread over the scene, and we are overpowered and taken prisoners...."

Col. James P. Major
(Photographic History of the C.W.)

Lieutenant William Marland, commanding a section of the 2nd (Nims') Massachusett's Battery, reported how he managed to save most of his guns. He wrote, "The enemy being within 400 yards of me, I opened on them with canister and percussion shell, which checked their advance and drove them to the right. I limbered to the front, and advanced to the fork of the road, which is about 100 yards; went into battery, and fire a few shot until all my support had left me. Finding it too warm, I limbered to the rear, and moved about 300 yards. Finding the enemy in my rear and on the right, I fired to the right about five shots, and was charged upon on three sides. A regiment came up on my left as support, fired one volley, and left.

"The enemy then opened two pieces of artillery on me at about 300 yards, killing 1 horse and disabling one caisson wheel. The cavalry still advancing, and no infantry to be seen, when they got within 30 yards I limbered up and started for the woods; here I ordered my cannoneers to draw their revolvers, and had quite a brisk fight; had another horse killed, 2 men missing (1 sergeant and 1 private); went through the woods, the enemy coming out in front and rear of men. As the bridges constructed across the bayou for passage of our troops were held by the enemy, it was necessary to charge through, which was accomplished, notwithstanding a cavalryman had mired and was taken prisoner near where the section crossed. I got through the enemy's lines without loss, and came up to the forty-sixth Indiana Regiment, and formed on their right." Marland was later awarded the Medal of Honor for leading his section to safety."[74]

Lt. William Marland
(Deeds of Valor)

Colonel Roberts continued his narrative of how the Confederate infantry broke the Federals' line. He wrote, "As the firing increased the 18th [Texas] was brought into line and also part of the 11th [Texas] before reaching the woods. There rushing through the gaps in a Bois de Arc hedge the line was promptly reformed without a halt on the outside of the field, when the enemy from a larger body apparently opened an increased fire directed mainly on my right, who being readily repulsed, a steady advance in line was made through the woods, the skirmishers being in vigorous action all the time, for one mile, when we met the advanced line of the enemy and Maj. [Nathaniel Jackson] Caraway having assembled our Skirmishers to the center Sheltered in a hollow, both sides commenced a general fire, which having lasted some time a charge was ordered, and very soon the enemy gave away. The firing having ceased a halt was ordered in the hollow which we were crossing and the men allowed to get in the hollow which we were crossing and the men allowed to get water and rest. The marching in line had been very difficult on account of the weeds, ditches and briars in the field, and the deep gullies, logs, brush, branches and curves of the bayou on our left, in the woods.

---

[74] Ibid, 371.

Marland's section of Nims' Battery fleeing the Texans at Bayou Bourbeau.
(Deeds of Valor)

"The 11th Tex. Regt. Encountered these curves in the bayou, and although some of the men crossed and recrossed the bayou, sinking in mud and water to their waists, it had been impracticable up to this time to keep the left of that regiment in line all the time, notwithstanding they exerted themselves to the utmost stretch of their remaining strength to do so. They followed however generally in good order by a march by the flank at the rear of the line so as to be ready to enter the line when the space allowed it."

Roberts then had Colonel Harrison of the 15th Texas send a company to relieve the advance skirmishers, who were seriously exhausted. "After a ten minute rest the line was promptly closed up and reformed, and an advance forward ordered. The whole line advance firmly up the ridge, where the firing of the skirmishers gave notice of the enemy's line, and then the firing commenced along the whole line on both sides, our men advancing their line by degrees under a constant fire of can[n]on and Small arms. While this was going on our line had advanced beyond the road nearly parallel with it, running through the woods and crossing the bayou at a bridge. Maj. Caraway, who had dismissed his Skirmishers to their place in line, informed me that a body of cavalry were posted up the road beyond the bridge to our left. "I directed him to take a part of the left wing of the 11th and form them under shelter of the timber along the slope of the ridge parallel with the bayou, so as to prevent their advance. Co. C of the 11th had been directed to fall in on the left when relieved as skirmishers, in anticipation of Something of this Kind; that being the only company of that regiment armed with Enfield rifles. Very Soon Capt. Hart came from that quarter and told me that there was great necessity for immediate reinforcement to guard against the cavalry. Capt. [Jack] Waterhouse's Company [I] of Lane's Cavalry reached there about that time. That however was not sufficient to resist the body of the enemy's cavalry. The firing of the enemy extending along our whole line, and therefore seeing no part of it from which any reinforcement could be drawn I ordered a charge. Our whole line responded at once and rushed towards the enemy, and continued it through the enemy's camp, they having fled before us. At which time our men were halted, faced to the rear and marched back to attack the enemy's Cavalry who had forced their way to our rear. They were immediately repulsed and scattered, and some few of our own men rescued whom they had taken prisoners."[75]

Colonel Harrison of the 15th Texas gave a more detailed account of the ending action when the infantry turned around and repulsed the Federal cavalry. He said, ". . . Adjutant [John B.] Jones informed me that we had been flanked by a regt of the Enemee [sic] Cavaly [sic] and they were about to charge us from the rear, when I faced my command by the Rear Rank and Charged them, producing among them before my line a scene of wild confution [sic], Men tumbling from Horses, screaming, Others throwing up their hands for mercy, Horses running wildly over the field without riders, others rooling [sic] and tumbling. Directly all was still. We pursued in the direction of the fleeing Eney [sic]

Pvt. Sam Jones, Co. E, 11th Tex. Inf. G.G.-Grandfather of the author. (Author's collection)

across the bayou through the timber where Genl Green had a Battery brought forward and our three Regts drawn up to protect it. Then an artily [sic] duel took place, the shell falling thick around us, . . . The Enemy having received heavy reinforcements [Gen. Godfrey Weitzel's division, 19th Corps], after remaining in position half [an] hour, Genl Green

---

[75] Roberts, 89.

ordered us to retire placing a cavly [sic] command in our rear."

A soldier of the 96th Ohio recalled the devastation suffered by the Federal soldiers. He wrote: "The ghastliness of the battle-slaughter every moment thickens. Heroic desperation sustains us in the endeavor to maintain our defense until help from some unlooked-for source may by chance arrive—for none is really expected. The gallant Burbridge rides up and down the tattered fragments of his brigade, directing and encouraging men who every instant prove themselves hero-hearted, ready to do all that may be done by mortals. But no aid comes, and stumbling to sertain [sic] death over comrades dead and dying, even the most dauntless falter. The moment is more than sublime, as each, without a murmur of the lip, asks his own soul, in agony, can we stay? Must we go?" [76]

Capt. Richard Coke of the 15th Texas Inf., wounded in action at Bayou Bourbeau, was a post-war governor of Texas.
(Library of Congress)

Burbridge explained the predicament in his report. He wrote: "My left now being totally gone, and the enemy's cavalry pressing heavily upon me, I gradually fell back through the ravine, so as to cover my train. The Eighty-third Ohio, which had been ordered back from the foraging expedition as soon as the action began, came up just as we were abandoning the ravine. Seeing that re-enforcements were coming up, so as to secure my left, I formed the Eighty-third Ohio upon the plain, upon which my shattered forces now rallied. My artillery was placed upon the left and the cavalry on the right. Here we checked the enemy until our support had come fully up, when the enemy retired. As soon as we could distribute ammunition to the men we advanced upon the enemy in the woods. General Cameron, upon my left, seeing that the enemy was

---

[76] J.T. Woods, Services of the Ninety-sixth Ohio Volunteers (Blade Print and Paper Co., Toledo, OH, 1874) 47.

disposed to offer but little more resistance, a cavalry charge was ordered through the ravine, and nearly 100 prisoners were captured. After pursuing the enemy a short distance beyond the ravine, we returned, picked up our wounded and dead, and fell back to Carrion Crow Bayou."[77]

Colonel Roberts said the Confederate infantry retired in good order, noting, "Having remained there under fire of can[n]on sometime, my command was ordered first to retire down west of the bayou, and shortly afterwards to withdraw in good order towards our train encamped one mile south of Opelusas [sic]. On arriving at the lane where the enemy piquets were posted as we sent out, the 15th Tex Regt retained by the Brig Genl Comdg and put in line to cover the withdrawal of our forces, and there remained under his immediate direction until the object was attained. The three regiments, taking into consideration their several positions during the whole action, which must have lasted three hours, were about equally exposed to the fire of the enemy; and behaved equally well."[78]

Colonel Wilburn H. King wrote of the 18th Texas Infantry's experience in the battle. He said, "The fighting was hot and in my own Regiment I lost nearly a third of my command, besides having five color bearers shot dead on the battle field. The sixth killed, also, supposed, until we [found him] barely alive, having been shot through the temple with a mini-ball. This made six color bearers shot down in succession in my Regiment during the engagement, five of whom were shot dead on the field in succession & the sixth one shot through the temple; and yet my colors never struck the ground!"

Pvt. Simeon J. Crews, Co. F, 7th Texas Cavalry
(Liljenquist Collection, Library of Congress)

---

[77] O.R., Vol. 26, Pt. 1, 360-361.
[78] Roberts, 90.

King noted there were bigger battles in the war, but the smaller battles battles should not be forgotten because ". . . many noble lives were lost and as many heroic deeds were done as on any of the bigger fields of battle." He also said by the end of the battle, his men were down to two or three rounds per man. King's other memories of the battle were seeing a 30-pounder Parrott shell from and enemy battery passing between him and General Green, and striking the horse Captain S.M. Hamilton was riding, behind the saddle. The animal was cut in two but Hamilton was unharmed. "The three infantry regiments made some reputation in this fight, my own particularly, being highly praised by Genl. Green for its coolness and courage in battle."[79]

Private Blessington of the 16th Texas, whose regiment was not actually in the battle, related in his memoir some occurrences, apparently related to him by veterans who had participated in it. He noted that Captain J. L.H. Stillwell of Company G, 11th Texas Infantry, was mortally wounded; Captain Richard Coke of Company K, 15th Texas Infantry, and a future governor of the state, was seriously wounded in the battle. Also seriously wounded were Captain William H. Christian, adjutant of the 11th Texas; Captain J.E. Hart of General Green's staff; and Major Caraway of the 11th Texas.[80]

Pvt. William P. Barnes, Co. A, 13th Texas Cavalry (Author's collection).

From the northern viewpoint, Colonel Guppey and much of the 23rd Wisconsin were among those swallowed up by the gray tidal wave overwhelming them. Guppey noted, at the end of the battle, "With one look at the Sixty-seventh [Indiana], another at the Eight-third [Ohio], then in front of our camp, and another toward General Burbridge, who was trying to form the flying men in rear of my regiment, I turned my

---

[79] Wilburn Hill King, edited by L. David Norris, *With the 18th Texas Infantry: The Autobiography of Wilburn Hill King* (Hill College Press, Hillsboro, Texas, 1996) 64-65.

[80] Blessington, 142, 143.

attention again to the advancing infantry of the enemy, and gave the order to fire as soon as it was within good rifle-range. Never was an order more coolly obeyed or better followed up. In ten minutes the regiment in my front was so doubled up that its men were 10 or 12 deep, and all mixed up, but still gallantly advancing. Two other regiments were also in the enemy's line, one to the right and the other to the left of that in my front, and each stretching beyond my flanks, and giving me a heavier fire than I could return. I then sent to General Burbridge for the Eighty-third Ohio, but he did not send it to our position. At this time I was wounded just below the left knee."[81]

Guppey's position then became untenable. He reported, ". . . I soon saw the long line of rebel cavalry (about 3,000 in number) charging across the prairie toward and around the camp, unchecked by the Sixty-seventh Indiana; in fact, the latter had then surrendered, as I afterward learned. Seeing that this cavalry would be in rear of me if I held my position longer, I commenced falling back toward the point held by General Burbridge while he was covering the removal of the train—fighting enough as we went to check the rapid advance of the rebel infantry. None of my men would have been taken prisoners if the cavalry had not by this time begun to get in our rear. While we were thus falling back, my wounded limb became so powerless, and I turned over the command of my regiment to Lieutenant-Colonel Hill, and attempted, with assistance of Lieutenant Stanley, to get off the field, but the enemy's cavalry was too near me, and the lieutenant and myself were taken prisoners by it. Afterward it took about 80 of my men, and among them many of the wounded. As soon as the enemy found that the baggage train was out of their reach, and that General Burbridge was prepared to renew the battle on the prairie, in rear of the Bayou Bourbeau, they left the field, hurried along by the shells from our artillery, and taking with them the prisoners they had captured."[82]

Bringing up reinforcements for Burbridge was Major General Cadwalader C. Washburn, acting commander of the 13th Army Corps. He reported, "While the fight was proceeding, the Third Division [McGinnis'] came up on the double-quick, but by the time they had reached the middle of the prairie, and 1½ miles from the scene of action, General Burbridge's command had been driven entirely out of the woods, while the rebel cavalry, in great force, charged through the narrow belt of timber on the left, and were coming down on his rear. By this time the Third Division had come within range, formed in line, and commenced shelling them, which immediately checked their further advance, while General Burbridge, who

---

[81] O.R., Vol. 26, Pt. 1, 365.
[82] Ibid, 365, 366.

had again gotten his guns into position, opened a raking cross-fire upon them when the whole force of the enemy retreated to the cover of the woods. Our whole force was deployed in line of battle, and moved as rapidly as possible through the woods, driving the enemy out of it, who retreated rapidly. I moved the troops upon their line of retreat about 1 ½ miles, while the cavalry pursued about 3 miles. My men having been brought up at a double-quick, were very much exhausted, and it was not possible to pursue farther."[83]

General Green was very satisfied with the outcome of the battle. In evaluating the results, he said, "The victory was complete, the fruits of which are about 250 enemy killed and wounded, 100 of whom are estimated to have been killed, and over 600 prisoners, 32 of whom were officers. Prisoners were taken from the following regiments: Sixtieth and Sixty-seventh Indiana, Twenty-third Wisconsin, Eighty-third and Ninety-sixth Ohio, First Louisiana Cavalry, and two batteries. Besides a large quantity of improved small arms and accoutrements, three pieces of artillery fell into our hands. We only had horses, however, to bring off one fine Parrott gun and caisson, most of the horses of the enemy's guns being killed. Two hours after our victory, General

A Confederate cavalryman
(Cdv, M.D. Jones Collection)

Weitzel, of the Nineteenth (U.S.) Army Corps, came up with a division of infantry of three brigades from Carrion Crow Bayou, 3 miles distant, and two regiments of cavalry. Deeming it imprudent to fight this large additional force, after a warm skirmish, I withdrew slowly and without loss, the enemy not attempting to follow me."

Confederate casualties in the battle totaled 22 killed, 103 wounded and 55 missing. By unit the following casualties were reported:

---

[83] Ibid, 358.

- 11th Texas Infantry, Col. O.M. Roberts, commanding, 4 killed, 15 wounded and 32 missing.
- 15th Texas Infantry, Lieutenant-Colonel James Harrison, commanding, 7 killed, 22 wounded, 5 missing.
- 18th Texas Infantry, Colonel William King, commanding, 10 killed, 40 wounded, 4 missing.
- 1st Partisan Rangers, also called Lane's Texas Cavalry, Major W.P. Saufley, commanding, 8 missing.
- 3rd Regiment (Arizona Brigade) Partisan Rangers, also called Madison's Texas Cavalry, Colonel George T. Madison, commanding, 1 killed, four wounded, 2 missing.
- 6th Regiment Partisan Rangers, also called Stone's Texas Cavalry, Lieutenant-Colonel Isham Chisum, commanding, 6 wounded, 1 missing.
- 4th Texas Cavalry, Colonel W.P. Hardeman, commanding, 4 wounded, 2 missing.
- 5th Texas Cavalry, Colonel H.C. McNeill, commanding, 6 wounded, 1 missing.
- 7th Texas Cavalry, Lieutenant-Colonel P.T. Herbert, commanding, 2 missing.
- 13th Battalion (Waller's) Texas Cavalry, Lieutenant Colonel Captain W.A. McDade commanding, 3 wounded.
- Rifle section, Daniel's battery, Lieutenant S.M. Hamilton, commanding, 1 wounded.[84]

Burbridge, in his report, said that the enemy left 42 dead on the field and were buried by his forces. Of his own casualties, the Northern general said there were 26 killed, 124 wounded and 566 missing. They also lost 36 horses, one 10-pounder Parrott gun and one caisson. "The engagement began at 12:30 p.m. and continued until nearly 3 p.m. Every inch of the ground was contested through the entire ravine, and both officers and men displayed the utmost coolness and bravery." He particularly cited Colonel Guppey, Colonel Owen and other officers for their gallantry, including Lieutenant Marland for saving most of his section of Nims' Battery.[85]

The total casualty toll for the Federals, given in the Official Records, was:

---

[84] O.R., Vol. 26, Pt. 1, 395.
[85] Ibid, 363.

- 60th Indiana, four enlisted men killed; one officer and 29 enlisted men wounded; two officers and 95 enlisted men captured of missing for a total of 131.
- 67th Indiana, two officers and nine enlisted men wounded; 13 officers and 187 enlisted men for a total of 211 casualties.
- 28th Iowa, two enlisted men wounded, which was their total casualties.
- 48th Ohio, a total of one enlisted man captured or missing.
- 83rd Ohio, four enlisted men wounded and one officer and 51 enlisted captured or missing, for a total of 56.
- 96th Ohio, 11 enlisted men killed; one officer and 22 enlisted men wounded; and 5 officers and 67 enlisted men captured or missing for a total 116.
- 23rd Wisconsin, six enlisted men killed; one officer and 36 enlisted men wounded; four officers and 81 enlisted men captured or missing, for a total of 128.
- 4th Indiana Cavalry, Company C, lost a total of one man captured or missing.
- 1st Louisiana Cavalry (detachment) lost three enlisted men killed; one officer and seven enlisted men wounded; and 27 enlisted men captured or missing for a total of 38.
- 14th New York Cavalry (detachment), two enlisted men wounded and one officer and two enlisted men captured or missing for a total of five.
- 2nd Massachusetts Battery (detachment), a total of two captured or missing.
- 17th Ohio Battery, one enlisted man killed, two enlisted men wounded and 22 enlisted men captured or wounded for a total of 25.
- The sub-total was 25 enlisted men killed; six officers and 123 enlisted men wounded; 26 officers and 536 enlisted men captured or missing, for a total of 716 casualties in all.[86]

It does seem strange that for all of the gallantry of the Federal officers cited by Burbridge, a total of zero were killed and just six wounded in the battle.

---

[86] Ibid, 359.

Battles of Stirling's Plantation & Bayou Bourbeau

First Sergeant T.B. Marshall of Company K, 83rd Ohio, wrote in his memoir of the aftermath of the battle, "Our camp was completely destroyed. What was not taken away was piled up and burned. As soon as the enemy had completed the work of destruction they departed after upsetting all our camp kettles, spoiling what little chance we had for dinner. The Colonel and Adjutant lost all they had, as did about all the line officers." He added, "After this disaster we moved back to Vermillionville bayou and finally, on November 8th, to Iberia. During this time we had frequent rains and the suffering and discomfort was very great, as we had no protection against the wet and cold."[87]

Officers of the 83rd Ohio: Col. F.W. Moore, left, Lt. Col. W.H. Baldwin, Maj. S.S. L'Hommedieu. *(History of the 83rd Ohio)*

Corporal Scott of the 67th Indiana wrote of the misery of being a prisoner of war. "On capturing us, for fear our main army would recapture us, they rushed us along at a lively gait all evening, until we arrived at Opolusus [Opelousas], just beyond which we were corralled upon the open prairie like a herd of Texas cattle, and when the sun withdrew his warm rays, and the cool November night came on, it found us upon this bleak prairie without shelter or blankets, and without anything to eat or drink; and last, but not least, the most of us were in our shirt

---

[87] T.B. Marshall, History of the *Eighty-Third Ohio Volunteer Infantry: The Greyhound Regiment* (The Eighty-Third Ohio Volunteer Infantry Association, Cincinnati, Ohio 1912) 115.

sleeves, having left our coats in camp when going out to meet the enemy." He added, "And now, when the cool evening began to close in, our situation was anything but inviting, while the prospects for the night were growing more gloomy, as we were now becoming uncomfortably chilly and surrounded by the rebel guards. We grouped ourselves together in little groups and lay ourselves down upon the cold grass—not to sleep, but to rest and think."[88]

EVALUATION OF THE BATTLE

The Battle of Bayou Bourbeau was similar to the Battle of Cedar Creek, Virginia, but with a big difference in the ending. On October 19, 1864, Confederate Lieutenant General Jubal Early's Army of the Valley caught part of Major General Philip Sheridan's Army of the Shenandoah by surprise, while Sheridan himself was absent, and thoroughly routed them that morning. But Early, unlike Green at Bourbeau, stayed on the field rather that securing the fruits of victory and leaving. By that afternoon, Sheridan returned and rallied his defeated forces and counterattacked the Confederates, completely routing them and winning the day. Early's shattered army retreated and gave up the valuable Shenandoah Valley permanently to the Federals.

But at the Battle of Bayou Bourbeau, General Green not only masterfully conducted the battle and engineered a solid Confederate victory, he also secured the fruits of victory and didn't risk a counterattack in which he would have been vastly outnumbered. That was a classic way for a much smaller army to defeat a much larger one, just as Stonewall Jackson did in the Shenandoah Valley Campaign of 1862. Lieutenant General E. Kirby Smith, commander of the Confederate Trans-Mississippi Department was among those impressed with both Taylor and Green. In a report to Samuel Cooper, Adjutant and Inspector General in the War Department in Richmond, he said, "I would respectfully call attention of the Department to General Taylor's late operations in Lower Louisiana. Cautious, yet bold; always prepared for and anticipating the enemy; concentrating skillfully upon his main force, holding it in check, and crippling its movements; promptly striking his detached columns, routing and destroying them, the enemy have been completely foiled in the objects of their campaign, and have fallen back for a new plan and a new line of operations. General Taylor has been ably assisted by his subordinates, and in this connection I would respectfully urge upon His Excellency the President the immediate appointment of

---

[88] Scott, 53.

general officers to his command. Not only will its efficiency be increased, but the services of the officers merit the promotion."

The Trans-Mississippi commander also brought to President Davis' attention General Green. He wrote, "Brig. Gen. Thomas Green, commanding the Cavalry Division, should be made major-general for his repeated successes throughout the operations in Lower Louisiana. He is a rising officer, and has displayed greater ability and military genius than any officer of his grade in the department. Col. A.P. Bagby, commanding Green's brigade, with Col. J.P. Major, Col. Horace Randal, and Col. J.W. Speight, each commanding brigades, should be promoted to brigadier-generals." It is evident from Smith's evaluation that the Army of Western Louisiana was, although small, one of the best in the Confederate Army. It was led by highly competent officers, and the fighting men were among the toughest in the Southern forces."[89]

General Cooper responded to Smith in a December 22, 1863 communication. He wrote that, in fact, J.P. Major had already been promoted to brigadier general and he requested more information about the various officers mentioned by him in his communication before acting on the recommendations. The Secretary of War, J.A. Seddon, added to the report that went to President Davis, "General Green might, I think be at once promoted, as a major-general in addition is probably wanted. The other promotions might await the answer to General Cooper's inquiry." After reviewing the various recommendations, Davis just added a note, "It is deemed better to wait for the present a reply from General Smith."[90]

For his own part, General Taylor was effusive in his praise for General Green. "Too much praise cannot be given to

Lt. Gen. E. Kirby Smith
Trans-Miss. Dept. Cmdr.
(Library of Congress)

---

[89] O.R., Vol. 26, Pt. 1, 384-385.
[90] Ibid, 385.

General Green and the troops engaged. The exact moment when a heavy blow could be given was seized in a masterly manner. I have so frequently had occasion to commend the conduct of General Green, that I have nothing to add in his praise, except that he has surpassed my expectations, which I did not think possible. This officer has within the past few months commanded in three successful engagements—on the La Fourche, on the Fordoche, and near Opelousas—two of which were won against heavy odds. His sphere of usefulness should be enlarged by his promotion to a major-general. He is now commanding a division of cavalry, and I respectfully urge that he be promoted. I also beg leave to repeat the recommendation previously forwarded for the promotion of Colonel Major. This officer has for some months been in command of a brigade, and has shown marked energy and ability," he wrote.[91]

---

[91] Ibid, 392.

5 Fighting Retreat

General Franklin began regrouping his shattered forces on November 4, 1863 and a slow retreat back to New Iberia. He would, however, be fighting all the way. Generals Taylor and Green were not letting up on the Yankee invaders in the least. Both Taylor and Franklin knew the overland invasion of Texas through Southwest Louisiana was a complete and utter failure. The bluecoat army was dispirited by the losses, and General Franklin knew it, writing, "I judge from the officer's information who went out with it that there is not yet a large force in our front, but one is gathering. I have brought all my force to this place [the Bayou Vermilion], and will give them a fight here if they will accept, which I do not believe." The Northern men felt they were being closed in on by hostile forces that were becoming increasingly threatening.[92]

General Washburn was unable to gain the return of the Federal officers who had been captured, most notably wounded Colonel Guppey. Washburn was, however, satisfied that the Federal wounded held by the Confederates were being treated well. General Burbridge retreated back to New Iberia, which had been fortified. The Confederates were harassing the Federal transports on Bayou Teche and Burbridge found out from his scouts that Confederate Major St. Leon Dupeire of the 1st Battalion Louisiana Mounted Zouaves was in command of 500 "French guerrillas," which was probably an exaggeration. He also revealed that Federal government agents were with the army, which was seizing cotton and sugar, to ship the confiscated goods to New Orleans. "All abandoned property is claimed by speculators," Burbridge said. "Major Cowan, First Louisiana Cavalry, has shipped 76 bales of cotton and 82 hogsheads of sugar."[93]

Meanwhile, the Confederates were still celebrating their victory. The

---

[92] Ibid, 344.
[93] Ibid, 362.

Texas cavalrymen of Waller's Battalion wanted to show their appreciation to Colonel Robert's and his Texas infantrymen for their part in the battle. George McKnight of Waller's Battalion read this tribute: "Colonel Roberts, I am requested by the men of Waller's Battalion, Texas Cavalry to deliver to your charge a drum captured on the battlefield yesterday by Henry Beasely, a soldier of our command. We tender it as a slight token of our high appreciation of the gallantry and general good conduct displayed by yourself and the infantry under your command.

"On that field your men compared favorably with the veterans of Green and Major's where achievements upon other fields had already won high renown . . . It furnishes gratifying evidence that the Texan is from habit a horseman and prefers the cavalry sword. Yet the son of the Lone Star State can accommodate themselves to any arm which the necessities of our country may require. . . The valor of your men reflects additional lustre upon the Lone Star escutcheon. This battle, fought by Texans alone, is another warning as to what (the enemy) may expect to suffer should he ever meet the sons of Texas upon their own soil. . .We present the drum without injunction in full confidence that when it shall beat for action, your brave men will not be slow to respond to the call."[94]

SKIRMISH BETWEEN CARRION CROW BAYOU AND BAYOU VERMILION

The next significant skirmish was on November 11. It was on that day that Brigadier General Albert L. Lee, commanding the Federal cavalry division, led the 1st and 2nd cavalry brigades from near Bayou Vermilion north on the road to Opelousas back toward Carrion Crow Bayou, about 16 miles. It was a reconnaissance mission to determine the strength of the enemy infantry, cavalry and artillery. Colonel Fonda with his 1st Cavalry Brigade of the 13th Army Corps, had 230 men of the 2nd Illinois Cavalry, 115 of the 3rd Illinois Cavalry and 110 with the 118th Illinois Mounted Infantry. The 2nd Cavalry Brigade, commanded by Colonel Thomas Lucas, consisted of the 87th Illinois and 16th Indiana mounted infantry regiments; and the 1st Louisiana (Union) Cavalry.[95]

After passing the town of Vermilionville, which is about 20 miles north of New Iberia, Colonel Fonda reported, "One squadron of Second Illinois Cavalry was sent forward as advance guard, and one squadron of the same regiment sent to the right, with orders to move on that flank at about a half mile from the main column. We had not gone far when the enemy's pickets were discovered; they fell back to a lane, to what appeared to be their reserve. Thinking they might make some resistance, I sent forward

---

[94] Edmonds, 305.
[95] O.R., Vol. 26, Pt. 1, 379.

another squadron of the Second Illinois. Nothing further of importance occurred on the march out.".[96]

The bluecoat horse soldiers continued on until they were within two miles of Carrion Crow Bayou. They halted and Fonda sent out a detachment of the 3rd Illinois to the right, and dismounted the 118th Illinois to support Nims' Battery. They remained in that position for about 30 minutes when they were ordered to retire by General Lee. But as the Federals were retiring, the Confederates began pushing back at their skirmishers. Fonda reinforced his skirmish line. After about four miles in retreat, one of the Confederates picked off Captain A.W. Marsh, who was in command of the 118th Illinois. Surgeon Madison Reece noted that Marsh was struck in his right scapulae and, "A column of blood was projected three feet from his body showing that a large vessel had been severed. . ." Marsh was dead by the time he fell from his horse. The gray jackets also attempted a charge on their enemies, but the bluecoats held the line and the Confederates were kept back. After reaching the Federal infantry, they eventually went back into camp.[97]

Col. Lewis Benedict
(Library of Congress)

Also filing a report on this skirmish was Colonel Lewis Benedict's, 1st Brigade, 3rd Division, 19th Army Corps. He reported, ". . . I marched my command about 1 mile north of Vermillionville, and took position commanding two roads leading east and west. Captain Trull, with his battery, reported to me, and took position, where the whole force remained until Captain Baker, of General Franklin's staff, brought me an order from General Lee to move forward to his support, as a superior force of cavalry and infantry was in his front, threatening him. I moved forward until I learned that he was retreating; then retired. Receiving a request to select a good position, where my men would be concealed, I did so, and waited. Our cavalry retreated to our rear, when the enemy advanced to the mouth of the road opening on the plain, and our artillery opened upon them with some effect. After an artillery duel of some twenty

---

[96] Ibid, 373.
[97] Ibid, 373, 374. Edmonds, 326.

minutes, their forces disappeared, and I received orders to retire. I did so, and again took position, in obedience of orders from General Lee, in a ditch near Vermillionville; but no enemy appearing, I was ordered to return to this camp.

"Our loss is as follows: One hundred and tenth [New York], 1 killed, 3 2 wounded; One hundred and seventy-third [NewYork], 1 wounded; One hundred and seventy-third [New York] 1 wounded; One hundred and sixty-fifth [New York], none. Total, 1 killed 5 wounded; all of whom were brought from the field." Little appears to have been gained by the excursion that cost the lives of Captain Marsh and a soldier of the 110th New York. Total casualties for the Federals was about 20 killed, wounded and captured. No figures are given for Confederate casualties in this skirmish.[98]

SKIRMISH AT CAMP PRATT

Another sharp skirmish was at Camp Pratt, six miles north of New Iberia, November 20, 1863. It was located at the southwestern side a Spanish Lake. It was established in 1862 as a training camp for Louisiana conscripts, and a small prisoner of war area. Several thousand conscripts were issued dirty white uniforms, given basic military training and assigned to Louisiana units at Vicksburg, Port Hudson and the Army of Western Louisiana. A Yankee prisoner of war, 2nd Lieutenant George C. Harding of Company F, 21st Indiana Infantry, gave a short description of his time there. He recalled after his capture, ". . . I was conveyed to Purgatory, 'Camp Pratt,' a camp of conscription and instruction, six miles from New Iberia, and fifty miles from the [Berwick] Bay. The camp itself was a collection of plank 'wedge-tents,' with here and there small editions of the stars and bars flapping their greasy folds in the breeze."[99]

Camp Pratt at the time of the skirmish was occupied by a detachment of about 150 cavalrymen of the 7th Texas under the command of Major Gustav Hoffman, a German-Texan from New Braunfels. There had been a large immigration of Germans to Central Texas in the 1840s and 1850s. While some to the German population of Texas opposed secession, many proved to be first rate soldiers for the Confederacy. The gray jackets were there to keep an eye on the Federal stronghold at New Iberia. Unfortunately for them, they were camped too close to that stronghold for their own good.[100]

---

[98] O.R., Vol. 26, Pt. 1, 368.
[99] George C. Harding, *The Miscellaneous Writings of George C. Harding* (Carlon & Hollenbeck, printers, Indianapolis, 1882) 322, 323. Winters, 156.
[100] Edmonds, 358.

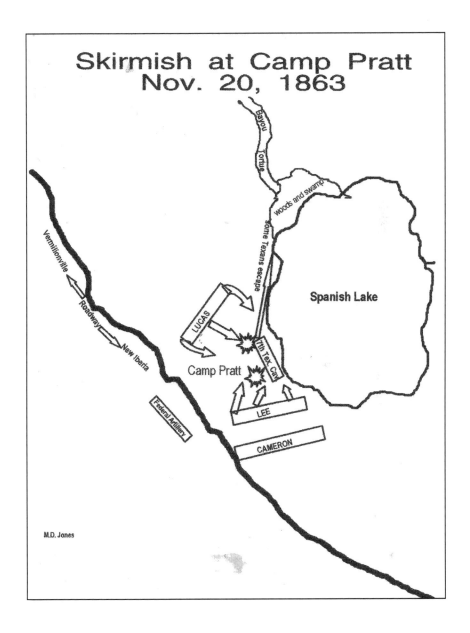

The Federals, still smarting from their trouncing at Bayou Bourbeau, were looking for an opportunity to go on the offensive and get even. General Lee asked for a chance to strike at Camp Pratt, and Franklin relented and let him stage an early morning assault on November 20. Colonel Lucas' 1st Cavalry Brigade,[101] and Colonel C.J. Paine's 3rd Cavalry Brigade, with a section of Nims' 2nd Massachusetts Battery, were given the assignment. Lucas, in overall command, moved out first at 2 a.m. on a road leading west from New Iberia. They then went north across the prairie that put them on the flank and rear of Camp Pratt.. At 4 o'clock that morning, Lee left with 300 cavalry, General Cameron's 1st Infantry Brigade and another section of Nims' Massachusetts Battery, moved directly up the road to Camp Pratt. "Just before day, at a point 1 mile south of Camp Pratt, my advance came on the enemy's pickets, wounded and captured 1, and drove the remainder in. I at once charged their camp with cavalry, the infantry moving rapidly in support," Lee said in his report.[102]

Hoffman and his Texans were thrown into confusion, and while trying to put up a resistance, were overwhelmed by Lucas closing in on their flank and rear as Lee pressed from the south. Major Hoffman and some of his men were able to escape through the woods in the north section of the lake. Also, Corporal William Miller, one of General Green's chief scouts, was able to escape. Others went among reeds in the lake and kept submerged except for their heads. Thomas C. Howard, adjutant of the 7th Texas Cavalry, aided other men in escaping through a gap in the Federal line, but was captured when he mistakenly ran into some bluecoats he had thought were Confederates.[103]

General Lee counted the spoils of his victory at Camp Pratt. "Our captures amounted to 12 commissioned officers, 101 enlisted men, 100 horses and equipments, and about 100 stand of arms of all kinds. His [Confederates] constituted the effective force of the regiment, which they claimed was the flower of their cavalry. The rebels lost 1 killed and 3

---

[101] The 1st Cavalry Brigade was reorganized November 7, under the command of Colonel Lucas. It included the 87th Illinois, 16th Indiana mounted infantry regiments and the 1st Louisiana Cavalry. Also on that date, Colonel Fonda was put in command of the 2nd Cavalry Brigade with the 2nd and 3rd Illinois Cavalry, and 11th Illinois Mounted Infantry. Colonel Charles J. Paine was put in command of the 3rd Cavalry Brigade with Co. F, 15th Illinois; Co. C, 1st Indiana; Co. C, 4th Indiana; the 2nd Louisiana (Union) Mounted Infantry; seven companies of the 6th Missouri, and six companies of the 14th New York.
[102] O.R., Vol. 26, Pt. 1, 370.
[103] Edmonds, 361.

wounded; our loss was nothing. I have to mention with commendation the promptness and skill displayed by Col. T.J. Lucas in conveying his command during the night of intense darkness to the rear of the enemy, and effecting so decided and perfect a co-operation with my attacking force in front. Col. C.J. Paine, commanding Third Brigade, Lieut. Col. H. Robinson, First Louisiana Cavalry, and Maj. Bacon Montgomery, Sixth Missouri Cavalry, are worthy of the special mention for their gallant conduct on this occasion. The infantry were, by the rapidity of events, denied any participation in the skirmish, but were eager and prompt in their conduct."[104]

Brig. Gen. Albert L. Lee Federal Cavalry Comdr. (Library of Congress)

SKIRMISH AT BAYOU PORTAGE

The Federals next decided to go after the camp of Major Dupeire's battalion of 1st Louisiana Mounted Zouaves at Bayou Portage, which had been harassing Federal transports on Bayou Teche. It was located at Dauterive's Landing about 16 miles northeast of St. Martin Parish. General Franklin assigned the difficult mission to colonels Lucas and Paine, with detachments of the three cavalry brigades totaling 650 men. Franklin estimated that Dupeire had between 200 and 300 men at that time. He suspected that Dupiere's men had recently cut telegraph wires to their army headquarters in New Iberia. Because of the rough, swampy terrain, the horse soldiers would have neither infantry nor artillery to support them.[105]

Dupeire had originally raised a battalion of two Zouave companies in the spring of 1862, apparently for the 1st Battalion Louisiana Zouaves, which had been serving in the Army of Northern Virginia. But because of the fall of New Orleans and following attacks on Vicksburg, they were assigned to that Mississippi River bastion. They became known as the 2nd Battalion Louisiana Zouaves, and were light infantry under the command of Major Dupeire. The Secretary of War ordered them to report to the Zouave

---

[104] O.R., Vol. 26, Pt. 1, 370.
[105] Ibid, 347, 362, Edmonds, 365.

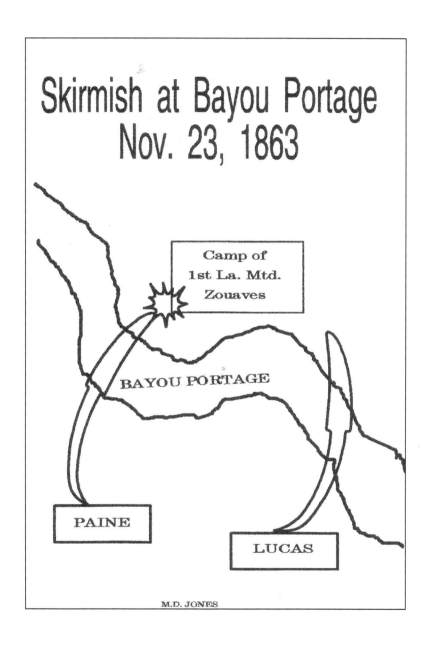

Col. Thomas J. Lucas
(Library of Congress)

battalion in Virginia in July, 1862. But Dupeire protested and they remained in Vicksburg.[106]

The men, who were enlisted from Louisiana's large French population, wore a uniform patterned after the French Army Zouaves, which included a red fez with blue tassel; short, dark blue jacket with red trimmings; a dark blue vest; red plantaloons; and white leggings with black leather *jambieres* (spats). The battalion fought in the Battle of Corinth, Mississippi on October 3 and 4, 1862. They lost two men killed and 14 wounded. At the Siege of Vicksburg, the Louisiana Zouaves were assigned to the right end of the Confederate battle line with Waul's Texas Legion at the Railroad Redoubt. There they fought from May 19-July 4, 1863 in that epic siege. After they were paroled at the end of the siege there, Major Dupeire reorganized them as the "Mounted Zouaves."[107]

Lucas and his command left New Iberia at 10 o'clock on the night of November 22 and the Saint Martinville Road. Colonel Mudd's command joined him when they were about six miles out of town and they proceeded on the road to Dauterive's Landing. They were then joined by Paine's command. "I sent Colonel Mudd down the road leading to Dauterive's Landing, with instructions to lengthen his lines along the left, skirting the road. On account of the fog, at the fork of the road he took the wrong direction, and reached the lake some 3 miles below the point indicated, failing to connect with me, though I have no doubt he made all possible exertion to co-operate with me." Lucas and his command spent the night searching for Dupiere with the only result of capturing four prisoners. When he finally got to the rebel camp at about daylight of November 23, he found Paine already in possession of it. He also learned that Colonel Mudd's detachment had captured Captain B.D. Dauterive and eight others.[108]

---

[106] Arthur W. Bergeron Jr., *Guide to Louisiana Confederate Military Units, 1861-65* (Louisiana State University Press, Baton Rouge, La. 1989), 154,155.

[107] Michael Dan Jones, *1st Louisiana Zouaves: Jeff Davis' Pet Wolves* (CreateSpace.com, Charleston, S.C. 2015) 68.

[108] O.R., Vol. 26, Pt. 1, 376.

Colonel Paine had left New Iberia at 11 o'clock on the night of November 22 and reached the vicinity of Dupeire's camp by 3:30 a.m. on the 23rd. "I marched down the bayou about 5 miles, and came on the enemy's pickets, about 10 strong. My advanced guards charged them and captured some; the rest took to the woods and escaped. The advance guard, which I then strengthened to 50 men, under Major [Bacon] Montgomery, Sixth Missouri, galloped half a mile farther into the enemy's camp, and captured many of them before they could escape to the woods. I scoured the woods with cavalry and infantry for 2 miles, picking up a few prisoners; burned the camp, with everything but the guns and property of use to us, which I brought away, including a number of horses; several of the enemy escaped, but excepting some of their pickets, it is believed, none with arms.

"I captured 25 enlisted men and 1 officer of Dupeire's battalion; 2 officers of the Eighteenth Louisiana; 28 in all, who have all been turned over to division provost-marshal. Two of the enemy were killed; none of our men were hurt; also the banner of the battalion, and the letter of presentation of the same, with the papers of Major Dupeire, all of which have been turned over to General Lee. The camp was that of Major Dupeire, Confederate Zouaves," Paine reported. Dupeire was not among the captured. He had been staying at a house at Dauterive's Landing with his wife, but had escaped the Federals by swimming to an Indian Mound.[109]

Col. Charles J. Paine
(Library of Congress)

Two days later, November 25, Colonel Fonda was leading a reconnaissance to Camp Pratt with portions of the 2nd and 3rd Illinois Cavalry when he came upon the enemy, charged them and had a five mile running battle. They succeeded in capturing one officer and 68 enlisted men. This marked the last significant action of the Fall 1863 Campaign in South Louisiana.

General Banks, in his report after the failure of the overland campaign to Texas, noted he didn't follow Halleck's recommendation of taking the Red River route, via Shreveport, to Texas because it wasn't practical at that time of year. But the approaches he took instead via Sabine Pass and across Southwest Louisiana both proved to be abysmal failures. He then

---

[109] Ibid, 377. Emdonds, 370.

explained the failures in his report: "The country between the Teche and the Sabine was without supplies of any kind, and entirely without water, and the march across that country of 300 miles with wagon transportation alone, where we were certain to meet the enemy in full force, was necessarily abandoned." He then added, "A movement in the direction of Alexandria and Shreveport was equally impracticable. The route lay over a country utterly destitute of supplies, which had been repeatedly overrun by the two armies, and which from Berwick Bay, with wagon transportation only, in a country without water, forage, or supplies, mostly upon a single road, very thickly wooded, and occupied by a thoroughly hostile population."[110]

Banks then justified his third attempt—the Rio Grande Expedition to Texas—which was at least partially successful, but too was abandoned for the disastrous Red River Campaign of 1864. ". . .I decided, as the only alternative left me for the execution of the orders of the Government, to attempt the occupation of the Rio Grande, which I had suggested on the 13th September as an alternative if the land route was found impracticable."[111]

It was obvious that Banks was not wholeheartedly in favor of invading Texas. He, along with Grant and Sherman, all agreed that moving against Mobile, Alabama, after the sieges of Vicksburg and Port Hudson, was the logical military objective. But Lincoln and Halleck ignored the advice of their military leaders on the scene, and pushed the Texas invasion for purely political and corrupt pecuniary—cotton stealing—reasons. While Banks has garnered most of the blame for the Federal failures in 1863 and 1864 in Louisiana, it is really Lincoln and Halleck who should have owned it.

---

[110] O.R., Vol. 26, Pt. 1, 20.
[111]

6 The Rio Grande Expedition

By mid-October, Banks was ready to give up on both the Red River and overland routes to Texas. He resorted to his last alternative, the Rio Grande Expedition. It was also the last phase of his Fall Campaign. The Rio Grande River was the natural border between Mexico and Confederate Texas. Since Mexico was a neutral country, trade between the Mexicans and Confederates was lucrative, but complicated, for both sides. The U.S. could not blockade Mexican ports and the city of Matamoros was on the border directly opposite Brownsville. In addition, Bagdad, a sleepy coastal village just across the border, became a boomtown during the war "crowded with merchants and traders from all parts of the world." Texas and the Confederacy could export valuable cotton, and import foreign goods, including weapons, uniforms and other military supplies. On the Texas side of the border were the towns of Brownsville, Rio Grande City and Laredo, which were also thriving on this trade.[112]

The Confederates didn't have much of a military presence on the border in the Fall of 1863. Brigadier General Hamilton Prioleau Bee was in command of Fort Brown, which had been built by Zachary Taylor in the Mexican War, in Brownsville. He had only about 100 men with him at the time. Born July 22, 1822 in Charleston, South Carolina, Bee moved with his family to the Republic of Texas as a child. His father, Barnard E. Bee, Sr., served as secretary for the commission to establish the boundary between

---

[112] James A. Marten, "RIO GRANDE CAMPAIGN," *Handbook of Texas Online*(http://www.tshaonline.org/handbook/online/articles/qdr04), accessed October 12, 2015. Uploaded on June 15, 2010. Published by the Texas State Historical Association.

the Republic of Texas and Mexico in 1843. When Texas became a state, his father became secretary of the Texas Senate. Young Bee served in the Mexican War as a private in Benjamin McCulloch's Company A, of Colonel John Coffee Hays' 1st Regiment, Texas Mounted Rifles. In October, 1846, he became a second lieutenant in Mirabeau B. Lamar's independent Texas cavalry company. Then in October, 1847, he was promoted to first lieutenant in Lamar's Company in Colonel Peter Hansborough Bell's Regiment, Texas Volunteers.

Bee started a political career after the Mexican War, serving in the Texas Legislature from the Laredo area from 1849 to 1859, including as speaker of the state House from 1855 to 1857. At the outbreak of war in 1861, Bee was a brigadier general in the Texas militia and was appointed to that rank on March 4, 1862 in the Confederate Army. His younger brother, Bernard E. Bee, Jr., graduated from the U.S. Military Academy at West Point, N.Y. in 1845, and also served in the Mexican War and was brevetted to the rank of 1st Lieutenant "for gallant and meritorious conduct" during the Battle of Cerro Gordo. Bee became a brigadier general of South Carolina troops in the War Between the States and gained lasting fame at the First Battle of Manassas July 21, 1861, when he rallied his troops with the famous phrase, "Rally behind the Virginian's! There stands Jackson like a stonewall!"—referring to General Thomas J. Jackson, known afterwards as Stonewall Jackson.[113]

Brig. Gen. Hamilton P. Bee
Cmdr. Rio Grande District
(Confederate Military History)

Banks said the expedition was twice delayed by storms, one before the transports and gunboats left Berwick Bay, and the other off Aransas Pass, Texas on the way. But he bragged in his dispatch to Halleck in Washington,

---

[113] Thomas W. Cutrer, "BEE, BARNARD ELLIOTT, JR.," *Handbook of Texas Online*(http://www.tshaonline.org/handbook/online/articles/fbe22), accessed October 12, 2015. Uploaded on June 12, 2010. Published by the Texas State Historical Association.

"I have the honor to report that on November 2, at meridian, the flag of the Union was raised on Brazos Island, which now is in our possession. It was occupied by a small force of rebel cavalry, which fled at our disembarkation without serious resistance. We left New Orleans on Monday, the 26th, at 12 o'clock, having been detained three days in the river beyond the time fixed for our departure in my last dispatch by a violent storm." He credited his failed movement at Sabine Pass and the Teche Country for the lack of resistance at the Rio Grande. "But for this, the landing we have effected would have been impossible. Our success is complete, and, if followed up, will produce important results in this part of the country," he said. "It is my purpose, after getting possession of the Rio Grande, to secure the important passes upon the coast as far as Pass Cavallo." The Pass is located on the central Texas coast and links Matagorda Bay with the Gulf of Mexico between Matagorda Island and the Matagorda Peninsula. It was a major export point for cotton, cattle, molasses, lumber, potatoes, and corn.[114]

Banks' expedition initially included almost 7,000 troops backed up by gunboats. He had three brigades of infantry from the 2nd Division, 13th Army Corps. The 1st Brigade was commanded by Brigadier General William Vandever, and included the 37th Illinois; 91st Illinois; 26th Indiana; 34th Iowa; 38th Iowa; 1st Missouri Artillery, Battery E and Battery F. The 2nd Brigade consisted of Colonel William McE. Dye, commanding the 94th Illinois,19th Iowa, 13th Maine, 20th Wisconsin and the 1st Missouri Artillery, Battery B. Other units with the expedition included the 15th Maine Infantry, Colonel Benjamin B. Murray, Jr.; 1st Engineers, Corps d'Afrique, Colonel Justin Hodge; 16th Infantry, Corps d'Afrique, Colonel Matthew C. Kempsey, and a Pioneer Company under Captain Alden H. Jumper.[115]

The landing of November 2 wasn't opposed, but also wasn't without cost to the Federals. The landing boats from the *U.S.S. Owasco* were swamped off the island and seven infantrymen and two sailors were drowned. Brigadier General T.E.G. Ransom was given command of Brazos Santiago and Point Isabel and took charge of the troops there. The 1st and 16th Corps d'Afrique were assigned to guarding the stores on the island at Point Isabel, and the rest of the expedition was to prepare to move up the coast and inland along the Rio Grande. Other immediate targets along the lower coast included Aransas Pass off Corpus Christi, and Fort Esperanza on Matagorda Island; and Fort Brown at Brownsville, about 30 miles inland

---

[114] O.R., Vol. 26, Pt. 1, 397. "CAVALLO PASS," *Handbook of Texas Online* (http://www.tshaonline.org/handbook/online/articles/rkc10), accessed October 13, 2015. Uploaded on June 12, 2010. Published by the Texas State Historical Association.
[115] O.R., Vol. 26, Pt. 1, 20,

Battles of Stirling's Plantation & Bayou Bourbeau

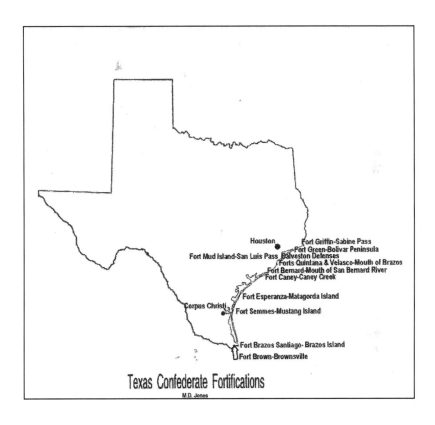

from the mouth of the river. Their forces would be boosted to 8,000 by the end of the month.[116]

But for General Bee, there was no hope for reinforcements anytime soon. Most of the available forces in Texas at that time were either along the upper Texas coast, including Houston, Galveston and Sabine Pass, or in Louisiana. Major General John Bankhead Magruder was in command of the District of Texas, New Mexico and Arizona with headquarters in Houston. Magruder had greatly fortified Galveston since taking it back from the Federals on New Year's Day. Other fortifications along the upper Texas coast, which Banks would have to take, included Fort Mud Island at San Luis Pass, Fort Velasco at the mouth of the Brazos River, Fort Bernard at the mouth of the San Bernard River; and Fort Caney at the mouth of Caney Creek. If he could muster enough troops to man theses forts, they could be a formidable barrier. There were approximately 40 Confederate camps and garrisons dotting the coast between Sabine Pass on the border with Louisiana, and the border with Mexico at the Rio Grande.[117]

VIDAL'S MUTINY

But for Bee, the crisis of a major Federal invasion was just another disaster with which he had to deal. Five days before he was faced with a serious mutiny by a group of Mexican volunteers, who had been keeping watch on Brazos Santiago. Bee's main force, Colonel James Duff's 33rd Texas Cavalry, was being ordered to report to headquarters in Houston. The mutineers, led by Captain Adrian I. Vidal, used the occasion to attempt to takeover Fort Brown and sack Brownsville. Duff began the movement October 28 by sending companies B, E and F to Houston. He remained with other companies at Fort Brown getting ready for the rest of the move. That afternoon, Duff wrote, "I dispatched Privates Litteral and [D.H.} Dashiell, of Company A, to the *Boca Del Rio*, with orders to Capt. A.I. Vidal, commanding a mounted company of six months volunteers, stationed as a picket at that point, to move into Fort Brown with his company on the next day, and report for duty to the commanding officer of that post." Along the way, the treacherous Vidal murdered Private Dashiell and severely wounded Private Litteral, who managed to get away and warn Bee and Duff. The traitors murdered several citizens before the mutiny was quelled.[118]

---

[116] Bill Winsor, Texas In The Confederacy: Military Installations, Economy and People (Hill Junior College Press, Hillsboro, Texas 1978) 108.
[117] Winsor, 108.
[118] O.R., Vol. 26, Pt. 1, 439.

Duff said Litteral had been shot through both jaws by Vidal's men and had to communicate by writing. General Bee found that he had only 19 men of Company A, 33rd Texas, and an unreliable company of State Troops to defend Fort Brown against Vidal. Be asked for citizens in the area to volunteer to defend the fort and town against the traitors, which brought his force up to 100. Bee said the trouble with Vidal occurred around the time of a rebellion going on between Mexican factions in Matamoros and the French intervention. Litteral told Bee that Vidal had his whole company plus deserters from Matamoros, consisting of some 60 men. "Fully satisfied, then, that Vidal and his whole company were traitors, I, with the able assistance of Brigadier-General Slaughter, Colonel Duff, Major [George A.] Magruder, Jr., of the general's staff, and Captain Winston, was enabled, with the cordial assistance of the citizens to get two heavy guns into a favorable position, and something like order and organization among the men." He also recalled the three companies of cavalry that had already left for Houston. Vidal and his men plundered ranches around Brownsville and then fled into Mexico. The swift action by Bee and Duff prevented the mutiny from proceeding, and 22 of Vidal's men were arrested in Mexico.[119]

Unidentified Confederate captain wearing a regulation coat.
(9th Plate Tintype, Author's Collection)

Vidal was born in Mexico in 1840 but after his father died, was taken as a boy to Brownsville, where he was raised. He had previously distinguished himself by capturing a Federal gunboat and crew at the mouth of the Rio Grande. With the coming of the Federals, he was commissioned a captain in the Federal Army in a command called Vidal's Independent Partisan Rangers. He and his units acted as scouts during the Federal occupation. Vidal became disenchanted with the discrimination he experienced from the Federals and tried to resign, but before his discharge, he and his men fled back to Mexico. He then joined the revolutionaries under Juan Cortina, who were fighting the French "Imperialists." Vidal was

---

[119] Ibid, 448, 449.

captured by the Imperialists in 1865 and executed.[120]

Responding to the Invasion

Just days later, Bee and his garrison were confronted by a much more serious threat—a major invasion of the Rio Grande Valley of Texas. As soon as he was notified of the invasion in the early morning of November 2, he dispatched Captain Richard Taylor and his 15 men of Company A, 33rd Texas, to the mouth of the Rio Grande to evaluate the seriousness of the threat. Bee also sent Captain Henry T. Davis and his 15 men of Company F, 33rd Texas, to Point Isabel to present him with constant information from that vantage point. Taylor reported back that he left with his men to the *Boca Del Rio* (mouth of the river) at 4 o'clock A.M., and then proceeded a half mile up the coast where he spotted a large vessel and several also inside the Brazos bar. Taylor and his pickets observed the Federals first landing 100 men on the tip of the island. The vessels then proceeded to the mouth of the river. That evening he withdrew to the ranch of Fermie Gonzales, who had been one of Vidal's men, and watched the movements that night of a large life-boat on the Mexican shore. As the sun rose on November 3, Taylor went with five men back to the mouth of the river and found the enemy had crossed over to the mainland with between 200 to 500 horses being herded by two soldiers and covered by 25 mounted men, who were armed and equipped.[121]

"Being unable to fight with the few men under me, I very quietly withdrew to the river, to watch their movements again at night. I encamped at noon at the Palmetto ranch, 9 miles above the mouth, and at 1:10 o'clock I discovered about one-half mile below, coming up the road, about 200 cavalry in full charge. I accordingly fell back to the chaparral, and made good my retreat, having expressed 2 men to your [Bee's] headquarters informing you of the rapid advance of the enemy on Brownsville," Taylor said.[122]

Also on the morning of November 2, Captain Davis with 19 men went to Point Isabel where he climbed to the top of the lighthouse there and discovered there were 24 vessels of outside the bar. He then saw two

---

[120] Jerry Thompson, "VIDAL, ADRIAN J.," *Handbook of Texas Online*(http://www.tshaonline.org/handbook/online/articles/fvi14), accessed October 13, 2015. Uploaded on June 15, 2010. Published by the Texas State Historical Association.
[121] Ibid, 443, 444.
[122] Ibid, 444.

Capt. Richard Taylor, Co. A, 33rd Texas Cavalry scouted the Federal landing on Brazos Santiago. (*On A Mexican Mustang*)

vessels move inside the bar and begin unloading men and supplies on the island. "I saw two regiments landed from those two vessels. In a short time troops were landing from a large vessel outside, besides a lot of stores. Two vessels during the evening moved off toward the *Boca Del Rio*." He and his men withdrew five miles inland and spent a quiet night. The next morning they returned to the lighthouse and found that two more vessels had come in during the night and had off-loaded a large number of troops and more supplies. He also saw one regiment landed on Padre Island. "Fearing that cavalry might be landed at *Boca Chica* to cut him off, and, having a very limited knowledge of the country surrounding the Point, I left for Brownsville with my party; had proceeded about 5 miles when I met an express from Colonel Duff, ordering me to join the command, then *en route* for King's ranch, which I did forthwith," Davis reported.

With this information, Bee determined he had no alternative but to retreat with all the public property he could load on wagons. He also sent out couriers to warn all the wagon trains carrying cotton to the border. On November 3, Bee got the warning from Taylor about enemy cavalry. He had only 80 officers and men with him to make the movement. They also carried with them an 8-inch siege howitzer artillery piece. Bee said, "Just as I was starting [with the wagon train], a courier came in from Captain Taylor

Confederate cavalry officer
(6th Plate Tintype, author's collection)

with the information that the enemy's cavalry were on the Palo Alto Prairie, 200 strong, and in rapid pursuit of him, and, if I intended to evacuate Brownsville, no time was to be lost. I immediately ordered the garrison to be fired, and in person superintended the burning of all cotton which was liable to fall into the hands of the enemy. At 5 o'clock I left Brownsville, and overtook the train at 9 o'clock that night, and proceeded to this place to send you this dispatch."

The property he couldn't haul off included 8,000 pounds of gun powder, which had been condemned. The fire and the explosion of the powder spread the conflagration to the town and burned a whole block of buildings. He noted that a large number of wagons were also crossed over the river to safety in Mexico. "By daylight on the 4th, I was joined by Captains Taylor and Davis, and then proceeded without interruption with the command to the point before stated [Santa Gertrudes]." Camp Santa Gertrudes was located in Cameron County a few miles north of Brownsville. Bee remained there for a few weeks before falling back as the Federals expanded their grip on the Rio Grande Valley.

He also wrote that the state militia troops had been disbanded before the retreat because he didn't have the authority to order them to go with his Confederate troops. Before disbanding them he asked if any would volunteer to go, and only one responded positively. He ordered the rest to stack arms and disband, which they did. Only a dozen Confederate citizens from Brownsville volunteered to go with the army. Bee also began accumulating reinforcements as various Confederates on outpost duty gathered around the beleaguered general. These included Captain Thomas Rabb's Company, which established a camp on the King Ranch about 35 miles southwest of Corpus Christi. Also, Bee was expecting to be joined by Captain J.H. Robinson's Company of the 33rd Texas, which had been on duty at Rio Grande City. The commanding general was quite happy with the performance of duty by Duff's regiment. He reported, "I bear testimony with great satisfaction to the good conduct of those troops—Companies A, B, D, and F. Their duty since the Vidal raid has been incessant and arduous, and not a single desertion has occurred." In addition, Lieutenant James Tucker, a member of P. Fox's battery who was in Brownsville on business, volunteered to take charge of the howitzer they had with them.[123]

BROWNSVILLE FALLS

In Houston, General Magruder received all the bad news from Bee, and began taking counter-measures. Magruder was a shrewd and experienced officer who seemed to shine his best when he was in a semi-independent command. He had scored an early Confederate victory when in command of the Confederate troops at the Battle of Ball's Bluff, Virginia. He then held back General Major General George B. McClellan's 100,000 man invasion force on the Yorktown Peninsula of Virginia in the Spring of 1862 for several weeks, although he had only about 11,000 men. But Magruder had also disappointed General Robert E. Lee during the Seven Days Campaign in 1862. When he was later assigned to command of Texas in the fall of that year, his star again rose as a semi-independent commander. Within a few months he had devised a brilliant and innovative plan to take back Galveston from Federal occupiers, which he did on January 1, 1863. He then built up defenses on Galveston to such an extent, it was never again captured by the Northern

Maj. Gen. J.B. Magruder
(CDV, author's collection)

invaders during the war. He strengthened the defenses all along the Texas coast, but didn't have the men and materials to adequately defend them all.

Before the invasion of the Rio Grande Valley, General Smith in Shreveport had wanted Magruder to mass the Texas State Militia to relieve the remaining Confederate troops along the coast. The Texas commander had been in the process of doing that but now used them to man a defense line he was creating on the Central Texas Coast to stop the invaders there before they got to the Houston-Galveston area. Magruder wrote Smith on November 21, ". . . I hope to be able to get troops west in time to save, if not Saluria, at least Velasco, at the mouth of the Brazos. It is highly

---

[123] Ibid, 434, 435. Winsor, 22.

probable, from the information received, that the enemy will attempt to take both of these places. I shall forward the information to Major-General Taylor, urging upon him the necessity of harassing the enemy in Lower Louisiana, as they may embark at any moment for the Texas coast, an event foreshadowed, I think, by their recent retreat toward Berwick Bay." He then added another dispatch on the same day, writing, "'Since writing to you in regard to the capture of Corpus Christi and Aransas, I received a telegram from Colonel [A.] Buchel, which I herewith inclose, clearly indicating, I think, the embarkation, of the enemy for the coast of Texas. Unless re-enforcements are sent me with the utmost dispatch, positions of vital importance may be lost. Upon the issue of the impending attack depends the fate of the heart of Texas, and I beg leave to most earnestly request the lieutenant-general commanding to order General Taylor to send to me, by rapid marches, such re-enforcements as he can spare from Louisiana."[124]

The Federals easily moved into Brownsville November 6, taking charge of the smoldering ruins of Fort Brown. They also set up a puppet governor of the state, the renegade A.J. Hamilton, and began recruiting renegades and deserters for the new 2nd Texas (Union) Cavalry. But Banks knew that if he was to take the invasion all the way up to Houston, he would need substantial reinforcements. He wrote to Halleck, "I earnestly entreat that we may be strengthened in our force by the return of so many conscripts, at least, as will fill up our regiments. I am certain that in New England and the West men will readily volunteer for service in Texas, if it is permitted. Unless we are strengthened, we may have to abandon the great advantage we have gained. We shall commence our movement to the Rio Grande to-day [November 4]."[125]

The 94th Illinois Infantry marched into Brownsville at 10 o'clock A.M. November 6; the 1st Missouri Light Artillery and the 13th Maine arrived at 3 o'clock that afternoon. They found Fort Brown burning, along with the property the Confederates could not move. "The conflagration extended to one or two squares of the town in the neighborhood of the barracks, which were also destroyed," Banks reported. He then accused retreating Confederate troops as having plundered the town, but Bee vehemently denied the accusation. Banks also noted that a rebellion in Matamoras had occurred after the arrival of the U.S. troops, and the governor there had been arrested. He made it clear he did not trust the Mexican revolutionaries and that the over-thrown officials were the true friends of the Lincoln regime.[126]

Banks next moved to secure the passes on the coast to the north of

---

[124] O.R., Vol. 26, Pt. 1, 432.
[125] Ibid, 398.
[126] Ibid, 400.

Brownsville, up to Matagorda Island. The bluecoats had yet to experience any serious resistance. On November 16, an expedition embarked to take the next city up the coast, Corpus Christi. Banks noted, "The troops on board were the Thirteenth and Fifteenth Maine, Thirty-fourth and Twenty-sixth Iowa, and the Eighth Indiana Regiments, and one battery of artillery, numbering in all about 1,500 men. We reached Corpus Christi the day before yesterday (16th), at 1 o'clock. We expected to be able to cross the bar at Corpus Christi with the [transport] *Matamoros*, one of the boats brought from the Rio Grande, and drawing 3½ feet of water, but we found the passage was impracticable, the bar being covered by only 2½ feet. We were, therefore, compelled to land our troops upon the coast [on Mustang Island]." The disembarkation was superintended by Brigadier-General Ransom (who commanded the troops during the day), and was commenced immediately upon our arrival, and occupied the night."[127]

Mustang Island Captured

General Ransom reported in more detail: "At sunset on the 16th instant, I embarked with the Thirteenth and Fifteenth Maine, Twentieth Iowa Infantry (two companies), First engineers, Corps d'Afrique, and two boat howitzers, through the surf near the south end of Mustang Island, and at once moved my force in a northerly direction up the beach, with a strong line of skirmishers in my front. Meeting no enemy, I moved rapidly, and by 4 a.m. on the morning of the 17th had made about 18 miles. I halted at this point, allowed the troops to rest until daylight, and again pushed forward.

"The enemy's skirmishers made a faint show of resistance about 1 mile south of their camp, when I deployed the Thirteenth Maine, and, advancing in line, drive them to their camp on the north end of the island, where the garrison consisting of 9 officers and 89 men, with a battery of three heavy guns, surrendered to me without further resistance, and unconditionally. I at once placed Col. Isaac Dyer, Fifteenth Maine Infantry, in command of the post, and made provision for the care of the prisoners and captured stores, which consisted chiefly of three heavy guns, the small-arms of the prisoners, one schooner, and ten small boats all in good condition."[128] They encountered minor resistance, which was quickly cleared away. The Confederate forces they found were Major George O. Dunaway with two companies of Texas State Troops and Captain W.H. Maltby's Artillery command at Camp Semmes. The Federal gunboat *Monongahela* shelled the fort and the Confederates returned fire for about a half hour, and then

---

[127] Ibid, 409.
[128] Ibid, 426.

Brig. Gen. Thomas E.G. Ransom
(Library of Congress)

surrendered. The Federals captured nine Confederate officers and 90 enlisted men, three heavy siege guns, a quantity of small arms and 80 or 90 horses. They also took a schooner.[129]

General Bee, who by that time had moved his headquarters to Camp San Fernando. He had accumulated just 355 men, including five companies of the 33rd Texas Cavalry, two companies of Texas State Troops, one company of the 8th Texas Infantry, and one company of cadets. They moved to Corpus Christi but upon arrival found that there had been no communication from the troops on Mustang Island. Colonel W.R. Bradfute, on November 18, mounted an expedition on the steamer *Cora* to see if they could rescue the Confederate troops there. It consisted of Captain P.H. Breeden's Company of the 8th Texas Infantry. Bradfute found that the small garrison of Camp Semmes had already surrendered.[130]

According to a report received at Confederate headquarters in Houston, the brief fight was a little more intense than Ransom reported. "The gunboats in the Gulf shelled our forces from their guns before the troops landed on the lower end of the island, came up, which was about 8 a.m. on the 19th. Major [George O.] Dunaway, of the State troops, is among the prisoners. . . The facts are all ascertained from persons who witnessed the fight . . ."

BATTLE OF FORT ESPERANZA

The next Federal target was Fort Esperanza on the northeastern shore of Matagorda Island. It was guarding Pass Cavallo, which was the entry to

---

[129] Ibid, 410.
[130] Ibid, 438.

Matagorda Bay. The pass separated Matagorda Island and Matagorda Peninsula along the central Texas coast. This bay was an important lane for shipping from the port town of Indianola, which ranked as the second port on the Texas coast. On the mainland, the Confederates were establishing a major encampment where reinforcements were accumulating at Cedar Lake Creek, also called Cedar Bayou, on the boundary between Matagorda and Brazoria counties. The camp was called Camp Buchel, for the post commander Colonel August Buchel of the 1st Texas Cavalry.[131]

The fort was one of the largest and best constructed on the coast. It was armed with eight 24-pounder smoothbore siege guns; one, 128-pounder Columbiad and a number of small field pieces. The weakness was that it was manned by only 500 men—detachments of the 8th Texas Infantry and 5th Cavalry, and Texas State Troops, all under Colonel Bradfute. Bradfute had quite a distinguished military record prior to the war. He was born May 23, 1823 in Sumner, Tennessee and served as a 1st lieutenant in Company E, 1st Tennessee Volunteers in the Mexican War from May 28, 1846 to May 1847. He was then promoted to captain and commanded Company H, 3rd Tennessee Volunteers from September 24, 1847 to July 22, 1848. He participated in the Siege of Vera Cruz, and the battles of Monterey and Cerro Gordo. Following that war, he served in the United States Cavalry, including as captain of Company I, 2nd U.S. Cavalry in Texas. This was the regiment specially raised by Secretary of War Jefferson Davis in 1855, which included Colonel Albert Sidney Johnston, Lieutenant Colonel Robert E. Lee, Captain Edmund Kirby Smith, and Lieutenant John Bell Hood. It fought both Mexican bandits and hostile Indians, including the defeat of the Comanches at the head waters of the Concho River.

Bradfute also had the unfortunate duty to shoot and kill a private soldier who had refused to follow a lawful order and struck the captain with a clenched fist. Bradfute was exonerated of any guilt by a court of inquiry. However, citizens appealed to the President of the U.S., who had him arrested and transferred to civil authorities for trial in 1858 at Fort Belknap. He was released on bail but his pleas for a trial were continually refused. When war between North and South began in 1861, Bradfute tendered his resignation from the U.S. Army on March 16, 1861, and then joined the Confederate Army. He had two brothers who fought for the North. He was married to Ann Elizabeth Bennett, December 5, 1850, and was described

---

[131] Ibid, 416. Winsor, 12. J. Barto Arnold III, "FORT ESPERANZA," *Handbook of Texas Online* (http://www.tshaonline.org/handbook/online/articles/qcf02), accessed October 16, 2015. Uploaded on June 12, 2010. Published by the Texas State Historical Association.

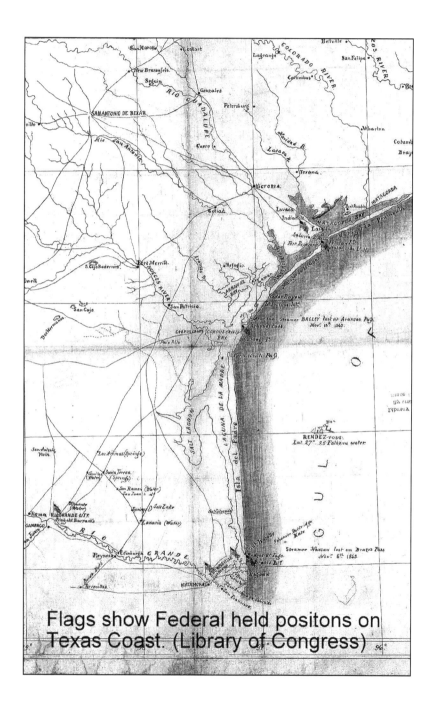

Flags show Federal held positons on Texas Coast. (Library of Congress)

as being 5 feet 10 inches tall, light hair, red whiskers, blue eyes and light complexion. Bradfute was said to have an impulsive temperament, but also was a brave and gallant officer.[132]

At Fort Esperanza, Bradfute received a communication from Houston headquarters on November 26. Captain Edmund P. Turner, assistant adjutant-general noted, "From the best information received at these headquarters, the enemy does not number more than 3,000 men, but should his forces be as large as you have reported, or should the fort become untenable for any other reason, you will withdraw your garrison, guns, and stores at the first opportunity, commencing at early dusk, spiking your heavy cannon, and destroying what you cannot move, and take post at Victoria, securing the rolling-stock and destroying the road, and informing General Bee, if not with you, of the result, requesting him at the same time to join you there." Fort Esperanza was also being sent reinforcements, Pyron's and Woods' regiments, but they were unable to secure transportation to the island.

Bradfute then replied that same day to Captain Turner in Houston: "Whilst I shall use every exertion for the best, I do not think that the transportation in this bay can be relied upon alone to supply any very large amount of troops. North winds prevent both steamers and sail-vessels from running, and, with a large amount of provisions at Matagorda, you may be without transportation when you least expect it. The two regiments awaiting transportation at Matagorda [Pyron and Woods] had better be ordered round by land; they are needed very much now. The enemy are making preparation at this time to advance up the island to make an attack upon us. If my force was larger, I could meet them down on the island, and not wait for them to attack the fortification. I think they have a land force moving up from Live Oak Point, 12 miles this side of Lamar. They should be met, so as to prevent this place from being flanked."[133]

Lieutenant J.A. Murray, the aide-de-camp of General Magruder who brought Bradfute his instructions and dispatches, gave a report on conditions in the fort a day before the battle began. He said the garrison had about 175 men who could do advance picket duty. Murray also noted the Federal cavalry scouts before the fortress were all mounted on fine horses that they had captured from Confederate cavalry on Mustang Island. "Colonel Bradfute seems confident of holding the fort, and says if he can get rations and assistance from the outside, that he can hold against any force," Murray said. The aide also said there were plenty of boats at

---

[132] Col. William R. Bradfute, article; Holman-Price Family File, Ancestry.com. Accessed Oct. 17, 2015.
[133] Ibid, 447.

Matagorda, including the Confederate cotton-clad *John F. Carr* and nine sailing vessels, which could ferry reinforcements to the island. "There is a very great necessity for a company or two of cavalry on the island. The cavalry that are on duty on the island are raw militia, that are driven in front of the enemy's pickets at pleasure; neither can they find out or are they sufficiently acquainted with troops to judge of the number or force," he added. On receiving this information, General Magruder formally requested that General Kirby Smith send him Green's and Major's crack brigades of Texas cavalry, along with their artillery, which were still in Louisiana, and which he said was no longer under a serious threat. He also called out all militia and all men capable of bearing arms in western Texas to report immediately to General Bee at Victoria to defend their state.[134]

Bradfute informed headquarters on November 27 that he was under attack. "The enemy have appeared in considerable force some 2 miles below the fort. From the best information received, they number about 3,000, including probably some 200 cavalry. We had a slight skirmish with them this evening, and it is supposed a few of the enemy were killed and wounded. No casualties on our side. The skirmish occurred some mile below the fort. Our force was withdrawn, and the enemy retired some distance down the island and to the west side. Their intentions are not yet known, but, from their numbers, I suppose they will soon make a vigorous attack. Our force here is about 500 effective men," he said in the report.[135]

Major General C.C. Washburn was in overall command of the Federals in the attack. He has two brigades, some 2,800 men, under the commands of General Ransom and Colonel Henry D. Washburn. A "Blue Norther" had blown in making the freezing cold weather miserable for all parties. Washburn overestimated the force in the fort as being from 700 to 800. "I soon discovered that the fort was a large and complete work, mounting heavy guns and that all approaches were well guarded." He added that the ground was a "level plain and the enemy works extended across from the Gulf to a lagoon connection with the back bay."[136]

Colonel Washburn's brigade consisted of the 8th Indiana Infantry, 18th Indiana Infantry, 33rd Illinois Infantry, 99th Illinois Infantry, and 7th Michigan Battery. The colonel's brigade was on the Federal right, proceeding up the beach toward the fort. On the 27th, they moved within 300 yards of the outer works of the Confederates. "The enemy now opened

---

[134] O.R., Vol. 26, Pt. II, 448, 449, 553.
[135] O.R., Vol. 26, Pt. I, 445.
[136] Ibid, 419.

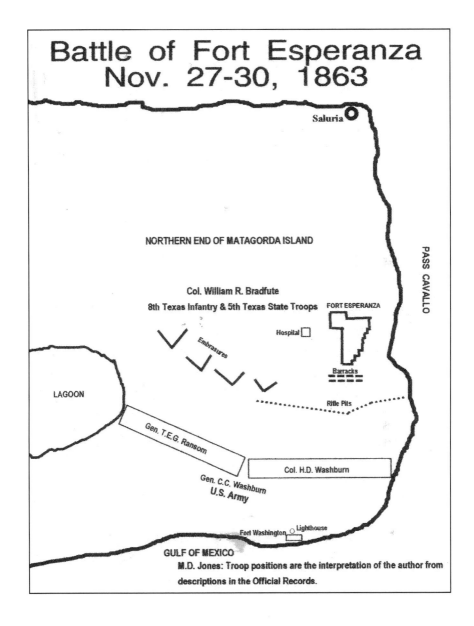

upon us from Fort Esperanza with his 128-pounder and 24s, throwing shells, but with little or no effect. Having found out the position and apparent strength of the enemy, by your order I withdrew my advance. During the night, a heavy norther coming on, we were unable to do much the 28th. The night of the 28th, Captain McCallister, of the Eighth Indiana, and Captain Hull, of the Ninety-ninth Illinois, both of whom had had considerable experience in that line in the rear of Vicksburg, with a fatigue party from each of the regiments in the brigade, under cover of the darkness, dug a rifle-pit from the sand hills on the beach occupied by us the first day, and running parallel with the enemy's works, 210 yards in length, sufficient to cover a regiment."[137]

General Ransom's brigade met the Confederate picket line at about 11 o'clock on the morning of the 27th. ". . . I placed my command in an advanced position indicated by General Washburn, on the left of our line and under cover of a slight rise in the ground. This afternoon and the following day were occupied in reconnoitering the approaches to the enemy's work, and was attended with occasional skirmishing and sharpshooting on both sides and occasional artillery shots from the enemy." Then on November 28th, Ransom said he had an earthwork built in advance of his left and opposite of the lagoon. ". . . where I placed Captain Foust's battery, supported by the Thirty-fourth Iowa Infantry, and opened fire on the fort at daylight on the 29th, continuing at intervals all day. In the meantime the Seventh Michigan Battery, of Colonel Washburn's brigade, had been advanced under cover of the sand hills on the beach, and opened upon the fort from the right of our line.[138]

The Federals charged the Confederate outer works at 4 p.m. on the 28th and took them. Colonel Bradfute followed General Magruder's orders and at 10 o'clock P.M. on the night of the 29th, he held a consultation with his fellow officers and they concluded that evacuation was the only option left if they were going save the men and as many arms and supplies as they could. They had received neither reinforcements nor supplies, and were in a hopeless position confronted by an overwhelming enemy force. The operation commenced and nearly all the men were moved safely to the mainland, except for six in the rear guard who were captured, and the body of one Confederate who had been killed in the skirmishing. The heavy artillery pieces that could not be moved were spiked. At 1 o'clock on the morning of the 30th, they blew up the fort. The Yankees had lobbed 155 shells at the fort, but only two men were wounded.[139]

---

[137] Ibid, 421.
[138] Ibid, 427, 428.
[139] O.R., Vol. 26, Pt. II, 464.

General Washburn said that his troops entered the fort an hour after it was blown up, and there was still a raging hot fire throughout the facilities. Since they hadn't been resupplied because of the weather preventing the transports from bringing them any, the Yankees found themselves hungry, cold and in dire straits. "Quite an amount of rations were found in the fort, which, if the fire does not consume, will prove a godsend, as we are entirely out," Washburn said. He also asked Banks for the 3rd Division of the 13th Army Corps, with which he said he could go to Houston. But then he added that his men were in poor physical condition. He also noted, "For the past two days my men have suffered greatly from cold, and I shall expect much sickness growing out of the exposure on these islands." The Federals lost just two men killed and 10 wounded in the battle.[140]

Maj. Tom Brackenridge, 33rd Texas cavalry, & 2 soldiers. (On a Mexican Mustang)

PREPARING FOR AN ATTACK ON HOUSTON

General Magruder expected the invaders to quickly march up the coast to Houston, but this approach turned out to be impracticable. The weather was bad, the bluecoats were still in need of reinforcements from New Orleans, and they would need more supplies. In addition, the land was much more barren and lacking in forage for animals and water for men,

---

[140] O.R., Vol. 25, Pt. I, 417.

than Southwest Louisiana had been. The Federals were having to haul their food, water and fuel all the way from New Orleans. Nevertheless, Magruder started concentrating all Confederate soldiers available, as well as Texas State Troops and civilian volunteers, at Velasco, at the mouth of the Brazos River, and to the south, the mouth of the San Bernard River and the mouth of Caney Creek. This triple line would eventually have about 6,000 men concentrated there on the middle Texas coast to stop any Federal advance on Houston and Galveston. Magruder had wisely chosen to fight at a strong natural defense line, rather than being cooped up in a fixed fortification that could be besieged and only end with the loss of both the position and men.

Caney Creek in Matagorda County, several thousand years ago, had been the main course of the Colorado River. Military engineers built four defensive positons at this location. These included Fort Ashbel Smith, on the west side; and on the east side Fort Hawkins, Fort Rugeley and Fort Sandcliffe. The armaments include a 30-pounder rifled Parrott and four 32-pounder smoothbore siege guns. Assigned to this post were the 4th and 5th regiments, Texas State troops. At the San Bernard River in Brazoria County, Magruder's engineers mounted two 12-pounder Parrott rifles and two 12-pounder smoothbore guns on the east bank. Major Henry Wilke with several companies of light artillery were stationed there.[141]

At the mouth of the Brazos River in Brazoria County, Fort Quintana was built on the southwest bank, just opposite of Fort Velasco. Fort Quintana was armed with two 18-pounder smoothbores, one 12-pounder, one 32-pounder naval gun and one 24-pounder smooth bore siege gun, *en echelon*. Fort Velasco, on the northwest bank, had six 24-pounder smoothbore siege guns, one 8-inch howitzer and one 32-pounder naval gun. Fort Velasco was built on the foundation of an earlier fort of the same name, which dated from the Republic of Texas days. Colonel Joseph Bates with his 13th Texas Infantry Regiment manned this large complex, supported by various artillery commands. The nearby town of Velasco also had a redoubt that mounted two 18-pounder brass guns, which were commanded by Captain W.S. Herndon.[142]

In November, 1862, Major J. Kellersberg, who was in charge of the engineering department, surveyed the area and filed a report on the defensibility of the coast between the San Bernard and Brazos Rivers. He wrote, "The coast from here [Velasco] to the San Bernard is easily defended, as there exists a series of lakes about 1½ miles inshore, extending from the Brazos to the San Bernard. The mouth of this latter river is very

---

[141] Winsor, 12, 31.
[142] Ibid, 35, 36 and 114.

difficult to access, having but 1½ feet of water at low tide and shifting sand bars for the extent of half a mile. I found there a 12-pounder gun served by a detachment of 6 men, which I ordered to be removed to the Brazos River, where the citizens try everything to put it in a state of defense." It is obvious why Magruder chose this area to make his main line of defense for the Houston and Galveston, from a coastal attack coming from the south.[143]

Kellersburg also noted that the citizens of the area were building an obstruction up river to block enemy gunboats that might try to navigate it. Kellersburg said he didn't have any faith in such river obstructions. However, he noted, "Within canister-shot of this veritable blockage is a battery of two 8-inch siege howitzers, built by order of Lieutenant Colonel-Bates. This work is exposed to the long range guns of hostile ships. I ordered some alterations to be made on it, both for strength and protection, and located a new battery of two 12-pounder siege guns on the opposite (left) river bank, out of sight of the ascending boats, and commanding the dam within canister-range. The planters here will furnish me with laborers and most of the material free of charge to the Government, and I therefore will erect for them a casemated battery for those two guns. All the work properly executed, nothing can pass this place; of this I have the fullest confidence. It was never even challenged by the Federals.[144]

Expecting a major battle, General Magruder moved his headquarters from Houston to the McNeel Plantation in Brazoria County along the banks of the San Bernard River. One of Stephen F. Austin's original "Old 300 Colonists," John Greenville McNeel built what was considered the most luxurious plantation home in antebellum Texas, named "Ellersly." It was a befitting setting for "Prince John" Magruder to conduct the defense of the state. He loved parties, ceremonies and luxury. The McNeel place was a large sugar plantation with many out buildings. The brick sugar mill resembled a turreted castle. The "big house" had 21-rooms and was located in an oak grove between two roads. It had mahogany stairs and bannisters and the ceilings were decorated with intricate plaster medallions. It was furnished with fine walnut and mahogany furniture.[145]

---

[143] O.R., Vol. 15, Pt. II, 854.

[144] Ibid, 854.

[145] René Harris, "ELLERSLY PLANTATION," *Handbook of Texas Online* (http://www.tshaonline.org/handbook/online/articles/ace02), accessed October 20, 2015. Uploaded on June 12, 2010. Published by the Texas State Historical Association.

The asterisks mark the Brazos & San Bernard rivers & the McNeel property.

(Library of Congress)

COTTON AND SKIRMISHES

The Federals never made a major assault on the Brazos River defenses, but there were plenty of skirmishes between the opposing forces. Back at Brownsville, General Dana concentrated on rebuilding the fortification there and confiscating cotton, which seemed to always be a major target of the Federals. He wrote on November 16, "I have sent into the interior 30 miles for some cotton which was reported as approaching the river above here, and I also expect a couple of lots in from a point 70 miles from here on the King's ranch road. The teamsters came to ask permission to bring it in, and security that they might sell it. I offered to pay their freight money ($4 per hundred) on their delivery of it if they would bring it in of their own accord. They consented, and have gone for it. The Thirty-fourth Iowa captured and delivered 39 bales on their march down to Point Isabel."

Dana also posted pickets 40 miles out toward Corpus Christi, and 27 miles out along the Rio Grande River. The pickets and videttes were also charged with scouting the countryside.[146]

On November 21, Dana sent out a force to the west to Rio Grande City, where Ringgold Barracks was located, under Colonel Edmund J. Davis, 1st Texas (Union) Cavalry Regiment. He had under his command 100 mounted men, 100 infantry and wagons, and 150 cavalry with one howitzer, proceeding both on land and on the steamer *Mustang*. Colonel John Charles Black of the 37th Illinois Infantry filed a report on the expedition. Black said seven of his companies were on the steamer and three were with the land forces and the wagons, which were for hauling confiscated cotton. By the 26th day of November the water level had gotten so low on the Rio Grande, that he sent a message to Davis with the land force to send back captured cotton to where the ship was stalled. The wagon train was also moving slowly and it was days before the cotton reached the steamer. The soldiers brought back 82 bales by December 1, and the *Mustang* started on the return trip to Brownsville.

They made very slow progress due to low water levels and they ran out of rations. He had to go into Mexico to the town of Old Reynosa to find more rations. Black found the Mexicans to be in an uproar over a raid by Americans led by John Travinio and 15 armed men. The Mexican National Guard, with some 200 men under Don Florentino, commandant, had mustered to invade Texas. Black offered to help him arrest Travinio, which he did on December 2, and found that the man was from a wealthy family and "very much a gentleman." He said he would submit the suspect to proper authorities. Black said they finally got three days rations at Edinburgh, Texas. He noted the regiment traveled 360 miles by water, 150 miles by land for a total of 510 in all. It seems obvious a major, if not primary purpose of the whole Rio Grande Expedition was to confiscate cotton for Northeastern textile mills.[147]

Camp Ringgold or Ringgold Barracks, which was renamed by the U.S. Army Fort Ringgold after the war, was built at the end of the Mexican War. It was the southern most U.S. frontier fort. Colonel Davis of the 1st Texas (Union), whom the Confederate Texans considered a renegade or Tory, was recruiting for the Federal Army, as well as confiscating cotton. He sent out another Texas Unionist, Philip Braubach, to do the recruiting, as well as seizing cotton throughout the countryside. Davis had no trouble taking Ringgold Barracks and occupying Rio Grande City. That cut off border trade from that point to Brownsville, but it was able to continue further

---

[146] O.R., Vol. 26, Pt. II, 413, 414.
[147] Ibid, 423, 424.

west at Laredo and Eagle Pass, Texas. The Federal recruiters were successful enough to form the 2nd Texas (Union) Cavalry, which was made up largely of Hispanics.[148]

A couple of notable skirmishes that occurred in December were the Battle of Norris Bridge in Calhoun County on December 26, and one on December 29 on the Matagorda Peninsula. The skirmish at Norris Bridge over Chocolate Bayou, occurred when a detachment from the 33rd Texas Cavalry was confronted by six regiments of Federal infantry supported by two companies of mounted infantry and artillery. Calhoun County is on the middle Texas coast opposite the northern end of Matagorda Island. Captain Richard Taylor, the same one who scouted for Colonel Duff at Brazos Santiago on November 2, was in command of a 40 man picket guard at the bridge on routine duty. The Federals were from Indianola, the winter quarters Yankees on that part of the coast. Brigadier General Fitz Henry Warren's brigade was tasked with a reconnaissance in force to learn the location, numbers and intentions of the enemy in their vicinity. Their destination was Port Lavaca, which at that time was just called Lavaca.[149]

The advanced Confederate videttes, as mounted sentries were called, first heard the pounding of hooves coming from Indianola in the early morning light. One of the Texans, Private Alexander Sweet, recalled, "There were about forty of us; and, as we could see at least three thousand infantry and a battery of artillery all coming rapidly in the direction of the bridge, it became very evident that something unpleasant was going to happen. As for the cavalry that chased us, they went back in a hurry; for, as soon as they got within two hundred yards of the bridge, a volley was fired at them which relieved them of any doubts as to our being militia, armed with shotguns. Our men were running to and fro, and everybody was asking where the captain was. He had gone to Lavaca the night before, to buy some flat plug tobacco—an unaccustomed and much-prized luxury with us then."[150]

Just as the Confederates were ready to break, Captain Taylor arrived. "He rode a large horse, and was dressed in an attractive buckskin suit, in the breast-pocket of which was exposed a plug of tobacco. We supposed, of

---

[148] Carl Moneyhon and Bobby Roberts, *Portraits of Conflict, Portraits of Conflict: A Photographic History of Texas in the Civil War* (The University of Arkansas Press, Fayetteville, 1998) 265.

[149] Alexander E. Sweet and J. Armoy Knox, *On a Mexican Mustang Through Texas, From the Gulf to the Rio Grande* (S.S. Scranton & Company, Hartford, Conn., 1883) 492. Calhoun County Historical Commission, "The Battle of Norris Bridge," www.calhouncountyhc.org, accessed Oct. 21, 2015.

[150] Sweet, 493.

course, that he would instruct us to retreat in quick order as possible. Imagine our horror and dismay, when, excitedly taking a large bite off the end of the tobacco plug, he raised himself up in his stirrups, and said, 'Fall in, boys. The war's been going on for three years, and we have not had a chance to smell gunpowder yet. Over in San Antonio they say we ain't anxious to meet the enemy. We will show them that it's a durn lie. I am not going to sacrifice life, or wade in human gore; but we will stay right here, and stand a few shells, anyhow. There ain't much danger until they get the range,' " he said. The long black line of Federal infantry kept coming and a man on top a nearby house said there were four guns in the battery. The men were now resolved to at least make a show of resistance. The battery then opened up when within 400 yards."[151]

On the Yankee side, a Federal soldier, Albert O. Marshall with the 99th Illinois Infantry, recalled, "Within four miles of Port Lavaca we came to the Chocolate River. The river here is crossed by a very fair bridge in the possession of a small band of the enemy. They had set it on fire and attempted to hold it until it should burn enough to prevent us from crossing. . . Our artillery was wheeled into line and opened on the enemy. Under cover of the fire of our cannon, some of our soldiers ran up, and using their hats for buckets carried water from the stream and put the fire out, almost in the face of the furious Texas rangers who had attempted to burn the bridge. Seeing that they were defeated, our opponents mounted their horses and rode away and were soon out of our reach. As we were unfortunate in not having cavalry with us, they easily escaped. With a couple of companies of good cavalry we could have captured them."[152]

Private Sweet noted the Confederates were along a fence line behind the bridge. He wrote, "Two more puffs of smoke, a cloud of dust appeared in the rear, and simultaneously about twenty feet of the fence was spread over the adjacent country. The sergeant [Jones] who had seen service in Virginia rested his rifle on the fence, and fired. The horse of the only mounted man about the battery reared, and fell over backwards. It was a four-hundred-yard shot with a musket—English Crown and Tower brand on it. We afterwards learned that the officer who rode the horse was shot through the thigh, and died in a few hours." Captain Taylor finally decided it was time to go. He ordered the men to mount up and go, which they did scattering out so as not to give the Yankee artillery a good target. He said they did hit a herd of cattle, mistaking them for a clump of rebels. "The shells continued to go over us as we ran. I rode alongside a lieutenant, who

---

[151151] Ibid, 495.
[152] Calhoun County Historical Commission.

Pvt. Alexander Sweet, left, is seen in this sketch riding alongside a lieutenant during their retreat from the bridge and was told to disperse. (On a Mexican Mustang)

was urging his horse onward by patting it behind with his sabre. We were then three miles from the enemy. I asked him if the way was hot enough for him. He shook his sabre at me, and said, 'Disperse, you damned fool! Keep way from me. Don't you know if we mass our troops the enemy will concentrate his artillery-fire on us? Deploy to the right, the farther the better.' " The men rallied at a creek six miles from the scene of action. "We rejoiced that none of were hurt: we did not wish to add to the bitterness of the fratricidal struggle," Sweet said.[153]

General Warren's brigade marched on to Port Lavaca, looted the town of all needed supplies and then burned the business district to the ground. They then retreated back to Indianola.

Another sharp skirmish occurred on December 29 as a Federal detachment of the 13th Maine Infantry under the command of Colonel Frank C. Hesseltine moved up the Matagorda Peninsula to gauge enemy strength. The Maine men were loaded on December 28 on the gunboat *U.S.S. Granite City*. They were then landed in small boats on the 29th on the peninsula at DeCrow's Point. They would soon encounter one of the crack Confederate units, the 1st Texas Cavalry under the command of Colonel August Buchel. The Texan commander was a German immigrant who had extensive military education, training and experience in a number of European wars, before coming to Texas in October, 1845. During the

---

[153] Sweet, 498.

Mexican War, he raised a company of Texas Germans that served as Company H, 1st Texas Brigade of Volunteer Foot Riflemen. Colonel Albert Sidney Johnston, who commanded the regiment, called Buchel's company the best drilled in the army. The company was a 90 day unit which disbanded before seeing any action. Buchel, however, was promoted to major and put on General Zachary Taylor's staff, on which he served for the remainder of the war.[154]

That morning the Maine men met only a few Confederate pickets, which they easily drove away. The pickets reported to Buchel that the Yankees landed beneath the mouth of Caney Creek and the force was made up on between 200 and 300 Yankees. Buchel ordered five of his companies of the 1st Texas and a detachment of Colonel Rueben Brown's 35th Texas Cavalry to saddle up and they went hunting for the invaders.

Pvt. Benjamin W. Varnell, Co. B, 1st Tex. Cavalry. (Liljenquist Collection, Library of Congress)

Buchel now led his men to confront the bluecoats, whom he found at 2 o'clock that afternoon. He then posted skirmishers in advance and pressed forward. Moving fast, the Texans were shelled by the gunboat *Granite City* but managed to keep pressing forward. The Federals fired as they retreated back to the neck of the bay and then built a haphazard breastwork of drift wood. To the Texans it looked like a very strong position with the gunboat backup. The Confederates outflanked their enemies, who just expanded their breastwork to a three sided barrier. After nightfall, the Texans and Maine men kept up a brisk fire until midnight. The Southerners then made a charge, but were driven back. A new gunboat, the *Skeeota*, replaced the *Granite City* and opened up on the Confederates. They fell back and the firing ceased for the rest of the night.

The next morning, Dec. 30, a heavy fog had settled over the area and didn't burn off until 10 o'clock. Buchel's men pressed menacingly around the Federal position, which had been improved and strengthened overnight. The *C.S.S. John F. Carr* came up at noon and began shelling the

---

[154] Stanley S. McGowen, Horse Sweat and Powder Smoke (Texas A&M University Press, College Station, Texas, 1999) 99, 117.

enemy position. Buchel's men vacated the area while the shelling was going on and at 3 o'clock Hesseltine was able to extricate his men from their exposed position, which the *Carr* continued bombarding. That night, the Yankees were picked up by the *Skeeota*. Hesseltine was eventually awarded the Medal of Honor for his actions during the skirmishing.[155]

By mid-December the Rio Grande Expedition was grinding to a halt, both because of the harsh winter weather, difficult terrain challenges and the over-stretched supply lines up and down the coast and back to New Orleans. Banks returned to New Orleans on December 15 to round up more reinforcements for his major assault on the Brazos River area defenses. But if Banks' thought the government in Washington would rally to his Texas campaign, he was sorely mistaken. President Lincoln was impatient for Banks to bring the rest of Louisiana under control before the 1864 presidential election. General Halleck was irritated that Banks had not given him prior warning about the Rio Grande Expedition and General Grant strenuously objected to it as well. In spite of its success, Lincoln and Halleck still insisted Banks take the Red River route and vigorously promoted that campaign. Halleck told Banks he couldn't count on any further troops from other departments for the attack on the central Texas coast, but could get troops from Major General Frederick Steele's command in Arkansas and Major General William T. Sherman if he would go up the Red River. There were also pressures on Banks to take the Red River route from New England textile manufacturers because of the enormous stockpiles of cotton then in the rich cotton growing area of West Louisiana and East Texas. On January 3, 1864, Major General Francis J. Herron took command of the U.S. Army forces on the Rio Grande, but those forces would be drastically reduced while preparations for the Red River Campaign advanced. But skirmishing and bombardment of the Confederate coastal fortifications would continue throughout the rest of the war. On January 4, Halleck renewed his past instructions for generals Banks, Steele and Sherman to take the Red River route and made it clear that was Lincoln's desire as well.[156]

FINAL THOUGHTS

The abandonment of the Rio Grande Expedition by the high command and the renewal the Red River option, led to an even greater disaster and defeat in the March-May 1864 Red River Campaign. It also led to the loss of

---

[155] McGowen, 117-119. Walter F. Beyer and Oscar F. Keydel, *Deeds of Valor: How America's Heroes Won the Congressional Medal of Honor Vol. 1* (The Perrien-Keydel Company, Detroit, Mich., 1902) 298-300.
[156] O.R., Vol. 34, Pt. 1, 1. O.R., Vol. 34, Pt. II, 41, 45-47.

almost all the tentative foothold the Federals had won on the lower Texas coast. Banks got all the blame but it is obvious that the lion's share belongs to Lincoln and Halleck. The Federals began drawing down the numbers along the Texas coast and by the end of the war were restricted to their initial landing site at Brazos Santiago. Colonel John S. "Rip" Ford was ordered by Magruder to San Antonio and raise a force to drive the Yankees out of the Rio Grande Valley. He raised some 1,300 men and began his campaign in March 1864. By July 30, Ford's "Cavalry of the West" had recaptured Brownville. The final land battle of the war was fought on May 12-13, 1865 by Colonel Ford's command and a Federal detachment from Brazos Santiago at Palmetto (Palmito) Ranch. It was a Confederate victory. The battles of the Fall of 1863 in Louisiana and Texas were serious distractions for the Federals and set back their war effort. But for the Confederates of Louisiana and Texas they were threats to their homes and families that could not be tolerated. It showed there was still plenty of fighting spirit in the Trans-Mississippi Department in the mid-war period.

APPENDIX I
SUMMARY OF PRINCIPAL EVENTS IN THE FALL CAMPAIGN OF 1863

Action at Stirling's Plantation on the Fordoche, La., Sept. 29, 1863.

Abstracts from "Record of Events" on the several returns of the Second Division, Thirteenth Army Corps, for September, 1863.[157]

DIVISION RETURN

September 1—Division in camp at Carrolton, La., and there remained until September 4, when it was reviewed by Maj. Gen. U.S. Grant, and ordered to be prepared to march immediately.

September 5—Embarked on transports, leaving the Thirty-eighth Iowa Infantry and all the sick, convalescents, and sufficient men to guard the camp and property, behind. It moves without tents, knapsacks, or woolen blankets, and sailed up river, arriving at Morgan's Bend on the 7th instant. A detachment of cavalry (about 200), under Major Montgomery, accompanied the expedition.

September 8—In the morning, the cavalry and Second Brigade were ordered out on a reconnaissance toward the Atchafalaya River, under command of Colonel Day, who met the enemy's pickets, and afterward found the enemy in some force, and, after some light skirmishing, drove them across the Atchafalaya River, and fell back 3 miles until morning.

September 9—The First Brigade, under Major-General Herron, started out and joined Colonel Day, when Major-General Herron proceeded in force to the Atchafalaya to reconnoiter; arrived about 4 p.m., and immediately began skirmishing with the enemy. Having ascertained position, &c., and orders being not to bring on an engagement, retired to the Mississippi. Marched 30 miles. Lost 1 killed, and 1 officer and 2 men wounded.

September 12—The cavalry force was ordered to the front to keep a close watch on the enemy, and the Nineteenth Iowa, Twenty-sixth Indiana, and a section of Battery E, First Missouri Light Artillery, were sent out some 7 miles in front, to strongly picket the country and support the cavalry, all commanded by Lieut. Col. J.B. Leake, Twentieth Iowa, where all remained, as ordered by department headquarters, watching and harassing the enemy. The rest of the division present on the expedition lay on the

---

[157] O.R., Vol. 26, Pt. 1, 326.

levee of the Mississippi, without tents, blankets, or change of clothing, with nothing transpiring of importance, until the 28th instant, when, Major-General Herron having received a leave of absence, Major-General Dana was assigned to the command of the division.

September 29—In the morning, the enemy, having crossed the river in force, surrounded Colonel Leake's command, and, after a desperate engagement, captured the largest portion of his men, with the section of artillery. Our loss is: Commissioned officers killed, 2; wounded, 4. Enlisted men killed, 11; wounded, 30; missing, about 350. It is impossible to obtain correct reports of the missing, as parts of each regiment are in Carrollton, and all regimental and company books are there.

September 30—Division still at Morgan's Bend.

October 3—November 30, 1863.—Operations in the Teche Country, La.[158]

Summary of the Principal Events

Oct. 3, 1863—The Union forces, under command of Maj. Gen. William B. Franklin, advance from Berwick Bay and New Iberia.
Oct. 4, 1863—Affair at Nelson's Bridge, near New Iberia.
Oct. 9-10, 1863—Skirmishes at Vermillion Bayou.
Oct. 14-15, 1863—Skirmishes at Vermilion Bayou.
Oct. 16, 1863.—Skirmish at Grand Coteau.
Oct. 18, 1863. Skirmish at Carrion Crow Bayou.
Oct. 19, 1863—Skirmish at Grand Coteau.
Oct. 21, 1863.—Skirmishes at Opelousas and Barre's Landing. Occupation of Opelousas by the Union forces.
Oct. 24, 1863—Skirmish at Washington.
Oct. 30, 1863—Affair near Opelousas.
Oct. 31, 1863—Skirmish at Washington.
Nov. 1-17, 1863—The Union forces retire from Opelousas to New Iberia.
Nov. 2, 1863—Skirmish at Bayou Bourbeau.
Nov. 3, 1863—Engagement at Bayou Bourbeau, near Grand Coteau. Skirmish at Carrion Crow Bayou.
Nov. 5, 1863—Skirmish at Vermillionville.
Nov 8, 1863—Skirmish at Vermillionville.
Nov. 11, 1863—Skirmishes at Carrion Crow and Vermillion Bayou.
Nov. 12, 1863—Operations about Saint Martinville.

---

[158] O.R., Vol. 26, Pt. 1, 334.

Nov. 18, 1863—Skirmish at Carrion Crow Bayou.
Nov. 20, 1863—Skirmish at Camp Pratt.
Nov. 23, 1863—Affair at Bayou Portage, Grand Lake.
Nov. 25, 1863—Affair at Camp Pratt. Skirmish near
Nov. 30, 1863—Skirmish at Vermillion Bayou.

Rio Grande Expedition, and Operations on the coast of Texas, Oct. - Dec., 1863.

Abstracts from "Record of Events" on the several returns of the Thirteenth Army Corps, for October, November, and December, 1863.

Return of Second Division

October 21—The Thirteenth and Fifteenth Maine Infantry were attached to the division by order of Major-General Banks, and the First Texas Cavalry, First Engineers, and Sixteenth Infantry, Corps d'Afrique, were ordered to report to Major-General Dana, commanding the corps and division, though not attached to the division.

October 23—The division embarked on transports, and dropped down the river.

October 25—Sailed for the mouth of the Rio Grande.

October 26, 27, 28, 29, 30, and 31 found them still in the Gulf, on board boats, *en route* to their destinations.

November 1—This division, under the immediate command of Major-General Dana, was on transports, lying off the coast, awaiting an opportunity to land, a storm raging at the time.

November 3—Commenced landing by lighters and small boats on Brazos Island, consuming several days, and losing two steamers and two schooners in so doing.

November 6—The Second Brigade, excepting the Twentieth Iowa, marched on, and occupied Brownsville. On the same day, the Twentieth Iowa occupied Point Isabel. The First Brigade, excepting the Fifteenth Maine, which remained at Brazos, marched on same day toward Brownsville, encamped on the Rio Grande, and marched into Brownsville on the 8th. The First Texas Cavalry marched in detachments, as their horses were unloaded, for same point—a long and tedious process, consuming several days. The First Engineers and Sixteenth Infantry, Corps d'Afrique, left at Brazos.

November 13—The Thirteenth Maine Infantry marched from Brownsville to Point Isabel.

November 14—The Thirty-fourth Iowa and Battery F, First Missouri Light Artillery, marched from Brownsville to Point Isabel, and the Fifteenth Maine, having crossed to Point Isabel from Brazos, the Twentieth and Thirty-fourth Iowa, and Thirteenth and Fifteenth Maine, and Battler F were placed under command of Brigadier-General Ransom, and proceeded up the coast by vessel, and landed on Mustang Island.

November 16—Marched up the island, captured a small fort, with heavy guns, prisoners, &c., and proceeded to Saint Joseph's Island.

November 28—Attacked a fort of the enemy, compelling them to abandon and destroy everything in it. This portion of the division is still absent, and no further reports have been heard from them.

November 30—The First Texas Cavalry, the Thirty-seventh Illinois, and a section of Battery B marched on Ringgold Barracks, some 200 miles above the Rio Grande, where a force of rebels were said to be; and are at this date, November 30, still absent. The remainder of the troops are at Point Isabel and Brazos Island, engaged in fortifying and holding those posts. Health of the troops generally good. A large amount of cotton and valuable stores have been captured and turned over to the proper departments, for which the various staff reports will account.

Additions:

Dec. 15, 1863—General Banks returns to New Orleans.

Dec. 23, 1863—General Warren's Brigade occupies Indianola, Calhoun County, Texas.[159]

Dec. 26, 1863—Skirmish at Norris Bridge, Calhoun County, Texas.

Dec. 29-30—Skirmish on Matagorda Peninsula, Texas.[160]

---

[159] O.R., Vol. 26, Pt. 1, 878.
[160] Ibid, 485.

APPENDIX II

ORGANIZATIONS OF ARMIES

Confederates

Army of Western Louisiana—Nov. 1863[161]

<u>Maj. Gen. Richard Taylor, Commander</u>

<u>Brig. Gen. Alfred Mouton's Infantry Division</u>

<u>Mouton's Brigade, Col. Henry Gray:</u>
18th Louisiana Infantry, Col. Leopold Armant
28th Louisiana Infantry, Lt. Col. William Walker
Crescent Regiment, Col. Abel Bosworth
10th Battalion Louisiana Infantry, Lt. Col. Gabriel A. Fournet
11th Battalion Louisiana Infantry, Lt. Col. James A. Beard
12th/16th Battalion Louisiana Infantry, Lt. Col. Franklin H. Clack
1st Louisiana Battery, Capt. F.O. Cornay
5th Louisiana Battery, Capt. Thomas A. Faries

<u>Polignac's Brigade, Brig. Gen. C.J. Polignac</u>
15th Texas Infantry, Col. James H. Harrison
17th Texas Consolidated Dismounted Cavalry, Col. James R. Taylor
22nd Texas Dismounted Cavalry, Col. Robert H. Taylor
31st Texas Dismounted Cavalry, Col. Trezevant C. Hawpe
34th Texas Dismounted Cavalry, Col. Almerine M. Alexander
11th Texas Battalion (infantry companies C, D, & E), Lt. Col. Ashley W. Spaight.

<u>Walkers Texas Infantry Division, Maj. Gen. John G. Walker</u>

<u>1st Brigade, Col. Overton Young</u>
8th Texas Infantry, Col. B.A. Phillpot
13th Texas Infantry, Col. J.H. Burnett
18th Texas Infantry, Col. Wilburn H. King.

---

[161] O.R., Vol. 26, Pt. II, 402, 465; 563-565. Edmunds, 408-409. Barr, 1-5; 29.

22nd Texas Infantry, Col. R.B. Hubbard
Halderman's Battery, Capt. Horace Halderman

2nd Brigade, Col. Horace Randal
11th Texas Infantry, Col. Oran M. Roberts
14th Texas Infantry, Colonel Edward Clarke
Gould's Battalion, Major E.S. Gould
Daniel's Battery, Capt. J.M. Daniel

3rd Brigade, Brig. Gen. William R. Scurry
16th Texas Infantry, Col. James E. Shepard
16th Texas Dismounted Cavalry, Col. William Fitzhugh
17th Texas Infantry, Col. Robert T.P. Allen
19th Texas Infantry, Col. Richard Waterhouse
Edgar's Battery, Capt. William Edgar

Green's Cavalry Division, Brig. Gen. Thomas Green

1st Brigade, Col. Arthur P. Bagby
4th Texas Cavalry, Col. William P. Hardeman
5th Texas Cavalry, Col. Henry McNeill
7th Texas Cavalry, Col. William Steele
2nd Cavalry Regiment, Arizona Brigade, Col. George W. Baylor
13th Texas Cavalry, Lt. Col. Edwin Waller Jr.
2nd Louisiana Cavalry, Col. William Vincent
Valverde Battery, Capt. Joseph Sayers

2nd Brigade, Col. James P. Major
1st Regiment Partisan Rangers, Col. Walter P. Lane
3rd Regiment Partisan Rangers, Arizona Brigade
6th Regiment Partisan Rangers, Col. B.W. Stone
1st Confederate Batter, Capt. Oliver Semmes

District of Texas, New Mexico & Arizona

Maj. Gen. John B. Magruder, Commander

Troops in Eastern and Western Sub-Districts, Dec. 31, 1863
[Central Gulf Coast only]
Eastern Sub-District

Brig. Gen. James E. Slaughter

Camp on Cedar Bayou, (Matagorda/Brazoria counties)
1st Texas Cavalry, Col. August Buchel
35th Texas Cavalry (nine companies), Col. Reuben R. Brown

Camp Wharton (Brazoria County)
Col. X.B. Debray
26th Texas Cavalry, Col. X.B. Debray
37th Texas Cavalry, Col. A.W. Terrell
McMahan's Texas Battery, Capt. M.V. McMahan

Fort Velasco (Brazoria County)
3rd Texas Infantry, Col. P.N. Luckett
13th Texas Infantry (six companies), Col. Joseph Bates
23rd Texas Cavalry, Col. N.C. Gould
Waul's Texas Legion, Capt. W.D. Hicks
1st Texas State Cavalry, Col. T.W. Jones
Infantry Brigade, State Troops (20 companies) Col. N.W. Townes

Camp Slaughter (Columbia, Brazoria County)
2nd Texas Infantry, Col. Ashbel Smith

Western Sub-District
Brig. Gen. Hamilton P. Bee

First Brigade, Col. P.C. Woods (Matagorda County)
2nd Texas Cavalry (nine companies), Col. C.L. Pyron
36th/32nd Texas Cavalry (ten companies), Col. Peter C. Woods

Second Brigade, Col. James Duff (Calhoun County)
33rd Texas Cavalry, Col. James Duff
35th Texas Cavalry, Col. James B. Likens

Unattached
3rd Texas State Cavalry (two companies)
5th Texas State Regiment (four companies)
Fulcrod's Cadet Battalion, Company A

Battles of Stirling's Plantation & Bayou Bourbeau

FEDERALS

Army of the Gulf[162]

Maj. Gen. Nathaniel P. Banks, commander

Great Texas Overland Expedition

Maj. Gen. William B. Franklin, in command of South Louisiana forces
13th Army Corps

Maj. Gen. Cadwalader C. Washburn

1st Division, Brig. Gen. Michael K. Lawler

1st Brigade, Col. David Shunk
33rd Illinois Infantry, Col. Charles Lippincott
99th Illinois Infantry, Col. George Bailey
8th Indiana Infantry, Col. Charles Parish
18th Indiana Infantry, Col. William Charles

2nd Brigade, Col. Charles Harris
21st Iowa Infantry, Col. Salue Van Anda
22nd Iowa Infantry, Major Ephraim White
23rd Iowa Infantry, Colonel Samuel Glasgow
11th Wisconsin Infantry, Major Jesse Miller

3rd Brigade, Col. Lionel Sheldon
49th Indiana Infantry, Col. James Keigwin
69th Indiana Infantry, Col. Oran Perry
7th Kentucky Infantry, Col. George Monroe
22nd Kentucky Infantry, Col. George Monroe
16th Ohio Infantry, Major Milton Mills
42nd Ohio Infantry, Major William Williams
120th Ohio Infantry, Major Willard Slocum

Artillery Batteries
2nd Illinois Battery A, Lt. Herman Borris
1st Indiana Battery, Lt. Lawrence Jacoby

---

[162] O.R., Vol. 26, Pt. I, 891-901.

7th Michigan Battery, Lt. George Stillman
1st Wisconsin Battery, Lt. Daniel Webster

3rd Division, Brig. Gen. George F. McGinnis

1st Brigade, Brig. General Robert A. Cameron
11th Indiana Infantry, Col. Daniel Macauley
24th Indiana Infantry, Col. William Spicely
34th Indiana Infantry, Lt. Col. Robert Jones
46th Indiana Infanty, Col. Thomas Bringhurst
29th Wisconsin Infantry, Lt. Col. William Greene

2nd Brigade, Col. James R. Slack
47th Indiana Infantry, Lt. Col. John McLaughlin
24th Iowa Infantry, Lt. Col. John Wilds
28th Iowa Infantry, Col. John Connell
56th Ohio Infantry, Col. William Rayner

Artillery Batteries
2nd Illinois, Battery E, Lt. Emil Steger
1st Missouri, Batter A, Lt. Charles Callahan
2nd Ohio Battery, Lt. William Harper
16th Ohio Battery, Capt. Russell Twist

4th Division, Brig. Gen. Stephen G. Burbridge

1st Brigade, Col. Richard Owen
60th Indiana Infantry, Captain Augustus Goelzer
67th Indiana Infantry, Lt. Col. Theodore Buehler
83rd Illinois Infantry, Col. Frederick Moore
96th Ohio Infantry, Lt. Col. Albert Brown
23rd Wisconsin Infantry, Col. Joshua Guppey

2nd Brigade, Col. William J. Landrum
77th Illinois Infantry, Col. David Grier
97th Illinois Infantry, Lt. Col. Lewis Martin
130th Illinois Infantry, Maj. John Reid
19th Kentucky Infantry, Lt. Col. John Cowan
48th Ohio Infantry, Capt. Joseph Lindsey

Artillery Batteries
Chicago Mercantile Battery, Capt. P.H. White
17th Ohio Battery, Capt. Charles Rice

19th Army Corps

Maj. Gen. William B. Franklin, commander

1st Division, Brig. Gen. Godfrey Weitzel

1st Brigade, Col. George M. Love
30th Massachusetts Infantry, Lt. Col. William Bullock
116th New York Infantry, Maj. John Sizer
161st New York Infantry, Lt. Col. William Kinsey
174th New York Infantry, Lt. William Watkins

3rd Brigade, Col. Robert M. Merritt
12th Connecticut Infantry, Lt. Col. Frank Peck
75th New York Infantry, Capt. Henry Fitch
114th New York Infantry, Col. Samuel Per Lee
160th New York Infantry, Lt. Col. John Van Petten
8th Vermont Infantry, Col. Stephen Thomas

Artillery Batteries
1st Maine Battery, Capt. Albert Bradbury
6th Massachusetts Battery, Let. Edwin Russell

3rd Division, Brig. Gen. Cuvier Grover

1st Brigade, Col. Lewis Benedict
110th New York Infantry, Col. Clinton Sage
162nd New York Infantry, Col. Lewis Benedict
165th New York Infantry, Lt. Col. Gouverneur Carr
173rd New York Infantry, Colonel Lewis Peck

2nd Brigade, Brig. Gen. James McMillan
14th Maine Infantry, Col. Thomas Porter
26th Massachusetts Infantry, Col. Alpha Farr
8th New Hampshire Infantry, Lt. Col. George Flanders
133rd New York Infantry

Artillery Batteries
4th Massachusetts Battery, Capt. George Trull
1st United States, Battery F, Lt. Hardman Norris
25th New York Battery, Capt. John Grow
1st United States, Battery L, Capt. Henry Closson

Cavalry Division, Brig. General Albert L. Lee

1st Brigade, Col. Edmund Davis
1st Texas Cavalry, Col. Edmund Davis
1st Louisiana Cavalry, Col. Harai Robinson
118th Illinois Mounted Infantry, Col. John Fonda
6th Missouri Cavalry, Maj. Bacon Montgomery
14th New York Cavalry, Lt. Co. John Cropsey

2nd Brigade, Col. John J. Mudd
2nd Illinois Cavalry, Lt. Col. Daniel Bush
3rd Illinois Cavalry, Capt. Robert Carnahan
15th Illinois Cavalry, Capt. Joseph Adams
36th Illinois Cavalry, Capt. George Willis
1st Indiana Cavalry, Capt. James Carey
4th Indiana Cavalry, Capt. Andrew Gallagher

Not Brigaded
87th Illinois Mounted Infantry, Col. John Crebs
16th Indiana Mounted Infantry, Col. Thomas Lucus
2nd Louisiana Mounted Infantry, Col. Charles Paine
2nd Massachusetts Battery, Captain Ormand Nims

Engineers and Unattached Units, Maj. David C. Houston
3rd Engineers, Corps d'Afrique
15th Infantry, Corps d'Afrique
22nd Infantry, Corps d'Afrique
25th Engineers, Corps d'Afrique
Independent Kentucky Infantry

RIO GRANDE EXPEDITION

First Division, 13th Army Corps

Maj. Gen. Cadwalleder C. Washburn

1st Brigade, Col. Henry D. Washburn
8th Indiana Infantry, Maj. Kennedy
18th Indiana Infantry, Lt. Col. Charles
23rd Iowa Infantry, Col. Bailey
33rd Illinois Infantry, Col. Lippencott

99th Illinois Infantry, Col. Bailey
7th Battery, Michigan Artillery, Lt. Stillman

3rd Brigade, Brig. Gen. Thomas E.G. Ransom (commanding detachments)
13th Maine Infantry
15th Maine Infantry
20th Iowa Infantry, (2 detached companies)
34th Iowa Infantry,
1st Missouri Artillery, Battery F
1st Engineers, Corps d'Afrique

Second Division, 13th Army Corps

Maj. Gen. Napoleon J. T. Dana, Commander

1st Brigade, Brig. Gen. William Vandever
37th Illinois Infantry, Col. John Charles Black
91st Illinois Infantry, Col. Henry M. Day
26th Indiana Infantry, Col. John G. Clark
34th Iowa Infantry, Col. George W. Clark
38th Iowa, Maj. Charles Chadwick
1st Missouri Artillery, Battery E, Capt. Joseph B. Atwater
1st Missouri Artillery, Battery F, Capt. Joseph Foust

2nd Brigade, Col. William McE. Dye
94th Illinois Infantry, Col. John McNulta
19th Iowa Infantry, Maj. John Bruce
20th Iowa Infantry, Maj. William G. Thompson
13th Maine Infantry, Lt. Col. Frank S. Hesseltine
1st Missouri Artillery, Battery B, Capt. Martin Welfley

Unattached Units
15th Maine Infantry, Lt. Col. Benjamin B. Murray, Jr.
1st Engineers, Corps d'Afrique, Col. Justin Hodge
16th Infantry, Corps d'Afrique, Col. Matthew C. Kempsey
1st Texas Cavalry, Col. Edmund J. Davis
Pioneer Company, Capt. Alden H. Jumper

Bibliography

Governor Henry Watkins Allen, edited and annotated by David C. Edmonds, *The Conduct of Federal Troops in Louisiana During the Invasions of 1863 and 1864*, The Acadian Press, Lafayette, La. 1988.

Ancestry.com

Anne J. Bailey, Texans in the Confederate Cavalry, McWhiney Foundation Press, McMurry University, Abilene, Texas, 1995.

Alwynn Barr, *Polignac's Texas Brigade,* Texas A&M University Press, College Station, 1998.

Bartlett, Napier, *Military Record of Louisiana: Including Biographical and Historical Papers Relating to the Military Organizations of the State*, Louisiana State University, Baton Rouge and London, paperback edition 1996.

Arthur W. Bergeron Jr., *Guide to Louisiana Confederate Military Units, 1861-65*, Louisiana State University Press, Baton Rouge, La. 1989.

Walter F. Beyer and Oscar F. Keydel, *Deeds of Valor: How America's Heroes Won the Congressional Medal of Honor Vol. 1,* The Perrien-Keydel Company, Detroit, Mich., 1902.

Joseph P. Blessington, *Campaigns of Walker's Texas Division*, State House Press, Austin, Texas 1994.

Calhoun County Historical Commission, Port Lavaca, Texas.

Paul D. Casdorph, *Prince John Magruder: His Life and Campaigns*, John Wiley & Sons, Inc. New York, 1996.

Confederate Military Service Records, Compiled Service Records of Confederate Soldiers Who Served in Organizations from the State of Louisiana. War Records Group 109. National Archives and Records Administration (NARA).

Edward T. Cotham Jr., *Sabine Pass: The Confederacy's Thermopylae, University of Texas Press*, Austin, Texas 2004.

David C. Edmonds, *Yankee Autumn in Acadiana: The Great Texas Overland Expedition*, The Acadiana Press, Lafayette, La. 1979.

Silas T. Grisamore, edited by Arthur W. Bergeron Jr., *Reminiscences of Uncle Silas: A History of the 18th Louisiana Infantry*, Louisiana State University Press, Baton Rouge and London, 129.

Handbook of Texas Online, Published by the Texas State Historical Association.

George C. Harding, *The Miscellaneous Writings of George C. Harding*, Carlon & Hollenbeck, printers, Indianapolis, 1882.

Wilburn Hill King, edited by L. David Norris, *With the 18th Texas Infantry: The Autobiography of Wilburn Hill King*, Hill College Press, Hillsboro, Texas, 1996.

Michael Dan Jones, *1st Louisiana Zouaves: Jeff Davis' Pet Wolves*,

CreateSpace.com, Charleston, S.C. 2015.

Michael Dan Jones, *Dick Dowling and the Jeff Davis Guards*, CreateSpace.com, Charleston, S.C. 2013.

Michael Dan Jones, *General Mouton's Regiment: The 18th Louisiana Infantry*, CreateSpace.com, Charleston, S.C. 2011.

T.B. Marshall, History of the *Eighty-Third Ohio Volunteer Infantry: The Greyhound Regiment*, The Eighty-Third Ohio Volunteer Infantry Association, Cincinnati, Ohio 1912.

Stanley S. McGowen, *Horse Sweat and Powder Smoke*, Texas A&M University Press, College Station, Texas, 1999.

Carl Moneyhon and Bobby Roberts, *Portraits of Conflict, Portraits of Conflict: A Photographic History of Texas in the Civil War*, The University of Arkansas Press, Fayetteville, 1998.

Thomas Reid, *Spartan Band: Burnett's 13th Texas Cavalry in the Civil War*, University of North Texas Press, Denton, Texas, 2005.

Betty Tyler Rosteet & Sandra Fisher Miguez, *The Civil War Veterans of Old Imperial Calcasieu Parish*, Louisiana, Southwest Louisiana Genealogical Society, Inc., Lake Charles, La. 1994.

Reuben S. Scott, *The History of the 67th Regiment Indiana Infantry Volunteers, War of the Rebellion*, Herald Book and Job Print, Bedford, Ind., 1892.

Alexander E. Sweet and J. Armoy Knox, *On a Mexican Mustang Through Texas, From the Gulf to the Rio Grande*, S.S. Scranton & Company, Hartford, Conn., 1883.

Richard Taylor, *Destruction and Reconstruction: Personal Experiences of the Late War*, D. Appleton and Co., New York, 1879.

Texas State Historical Association. *The Southwestern Historical Quarterly, Volume 67, July 1963 - April, 1964*, H. Bailey Carroll, editor, Journal/Magazine/Newsletter, 1964

War of the Rebellion: A Compilation of the Union and Confederate Armies (1880-1901); Series 1, Vols. 15, 26 and 34. U.S. Government Printing Office, Washington, D.C.

Ezra J. Warner, *General in Gray: Lives of the Confederate Commanders*, Louisiana State University Press, Baton Rouge, La. 1987.

Bill Winsor, *Texas In The Confederacy: Military Installations, Economy and People*, Hill Junior College Press, Hillsboro, Texas 1978.

Ralph A. Wooster, *Civil War Texas*, Texas State Historical Association, Austin, Texas 1999.

John D. Winters, *The Civil War in Louisiana*, Louisiana State University Press, Baton Rouge and London, 1963.

Index

1st Conf. Batt., 20
1st Confederate Battery, 43
1st La. Mtd. Zouaves, 75, 81
1st Missouri Lt. Art., 16, 96
1st Tex. (Union) Cav., 109
1st Tex. Cav., 112
2nd Ill. Cav., 16, 76
2nd La. Cav., 34, 35, 41
2nd Louisiana Zouaves, 81
2nd Mass. Batt., 55, 60
2nd Mass. Lt. Art., 35
2nd R. I. Cav., 55
2nd Tex. (Union) Cav., 96
3rd Cav, Reg't, Az. Brig., 20
3rd Reg't., Az. Brig., 33
4th Tex. Cav., 20, 23, 43
5th Tex. Cav., 20, 23, 44, 47, 53
6th Missouri Cav., 21, 81, 84
6th Missouri Cav. Bn., 16
7th Tex. Cav., 20, 23, 44, 57, 78
7th Tex. Inf., 52
8th Tex. Inf., 98
10th Bn. La. Inf., 19
11th Bn. La. Inf., 19
11th Bn. Tex. Vols., 13, 19
11th Tex. Inf. Reg't., 51, 57, 58, 61, 62, 66
12th/16th Bn. La. Inf., 19, 23, 29
13th Army Corps, 10, 13
13th Bn. Tex. Cav., 23
13th Maine Inf., 97, 112
13th Tex. Inf., 106
14th N.Y. Cav., 55
15th Tex. Inf., 19, 23, 45, 51, 57, 58, 62, 65, 66
17th Ohio Batt., 55
17th Tex. Dism. Cav., 45
18th La. Inf., 19
18th Tex. Inf., 51, 57, 58, 61, 65
19th Army Corps, 10, 41, 44, 77
19th Iowa Infantry, 16, 19, 21, 28, 30
21st Ind. Inf., 78
22nd Tex. Dism. Cav., 45
23rd Wis. Inf., 55, 58, 66
24th La. Inf., 19
26th Indiana Infantry, 16, 21, 30
28th La. Inf., 19
29th Wis. Inf., 47
31st Tex. Dism. Cav., 19
33rd Tex. Cav., 90, 94, 110
34th Iowa Infantry, 16
34th Tex. Dism. Cav., 45
35th Tex. (Brown's) Cav., 113
37th Ill. Inf., 109
37th Illinois Infantry, 33
60th Ind. Inf., 55, 59
67th Ind. Inf., 13, 55, 60, 71
83rd Ohio Inf., 55, 71
94th Ill. Inf., 96
96th Ohio Inf., 44, 55, 64
99th Ill. Inf., 111
118th Ill. Mtd. Inf., 45, 77
Allen, Henry W., 37
Andrus, Elair, 26
Armant, Leopold, 19
Bagby, Arthur P., 51, 52, 57, 73
Banks, Nathaniel P., 9, 11, 84, 87, 96
Barney, William, 47
Bates, Joseph, 106
Battle of Bayou Bourbeau, 53, 72
Battle of Bisland, 53
Battle of Buzzard's Prairie, 41
Battle of Cedar Creek, Va., 72

Battle of Farmington, Miss., 34
Battle of Galveston, 52
Battle of Norris Bridge, 110
Battle of Opelousas, 45
Battle of Shiloh, 34
Battle of Stirling's Plantation, 17
Beard, James, 19
Beasley, Henry, 76
Beaumont, Jacob, 30
Bee, Bernard, 87
Bee, Hamilton P., 86, 90, 92, 96
Benedict, Lewis, 77
Black, John C., 109
Blessington, Joseph P., 41, 54, 66
Boone, Hannibal H., 19, 32
Bosworth, Abel, 19
Bradfute, 104
Bradfute, Hamilton P., 102
Bradfute, William R., 98, 99
Brown, Albert, 55
Brown, Reuben, 113
Bruce, John, 28
Bryan, J.K., 25
Buchel, August, 112
Buehler, Theodore, 55, 60
Burbridge, Stephen, 43, 54, 58, 67, 75
Burrell, Robert, 25, 30
C.S.S. John F. Carr, 102, 113
Camp Pratt, 78
Camp Ringgold, 109
Caraway, Nathaniel J., 61
Carriere, Ozeme, 48
Christian, William H., 66
Clack, Franklin H., 19
Coke, Richard, 66
Cooper, Samuel, 73
Coupland, Sam H., 57
Cropsey, John, 55

Dana, N.J.T., 16, 17, 32, 37, 108
Daniel, John W., 19
Daniel's Tex. Batt., 57
Dashiell, D.H., 90
Davis, Edmund, 43
Davis, Henry T., 92
Davis, Jefferson, 73
Dowling, Dick, 9
Duff, James, 90
Dunaway, George O., 97
Dungan, James I., 19, 27
Dupeire, Saint Leon, 81
Dupeire, St. Leon, 75, 81, 84
Dye, William, 88
Dyer, Isaac, 97
Early, Jubal, 72
Ford, John S., 115
Fort Ashbel Smith, 106
Fort Brown, 90, 96
Fort Caney, 90
Fort Esperanza, 98, 101, 104
Fort Hawkins, 106
Fort Mud Island, 90
Fort Quintana, 106
Fort Velasco, 90, 106
Fournet, Valsin, 19
Franklin, William B., 10, 41, 48, 75
Goelzer, Augustus, 55
Gray, Henry, 19
Green, Thomas, 12, 20, 28, 30, 43, 49, 51, 58, 59, 66, 68, 72, 76
Grover, Cuvier, 10, 43
Guppey, Joshua, 55, 58, 66
Hamilton, A.J., 96
Hamilton, Samuel M., 57, 66
Haney, James A., 30
Hardeman, William P., 43
Harding, George C., 78

Harrison, James E., 24, 32, 51
Hart, J.E., 57
Hart, J.H., 66
Herndon, W.S., 106
Herron, Francis J., 16, 114
Hesseltine, Frank C., 112
Hoffman, Gustav, 78
Hume, P.G., 57
Irvine, J.B., 25
Johnson, F.W., 57
Jones, J.B., 26
Jones, James H., 51
Jones, John B., 63
Jones, Samuel D., 63
Kellersberg, J., 106
Kent, Ambrose D., 30
Kent, Silas, 31
King, Wilburn H., 51, 65
Kirby, Allen, 57
Leake, J.B., 16, 18, 21, 30
Lee, Albert L., 10, 76
Long, James M., 30
Lucas, T.J., 81, 83
Madison, George T., 20
Magruder, John B., 35, 36, 95, 105, 107
Major, James P., 20, 36, 51, 57, 59, 73, 76
Malone, Frederick J., 19
Marland, William, 55, 60
Marsh, A.W., 77
Marshall, Albert O., 111
Marshall, T.B., 71
McClure, Levi, 30
McFadden, Andrew, 30
McKee, Sam, 26, 30
McKnight, George, 76
McNeel, John G., 107
Montgomery, Bacon, 55, 84
Moore, Frederick, 55
Mouton, Alfred, 11, 19, 20, 35
Mouton's Infantry Division, 41
Murray, J.A., 101
Nettles, Timothy D., 53
Nims, Ormond, 44
O'Bryan, George W., 13, 17, 18, 21, 28, 40
O'Bryan, Robert P., 25, 28
Ord, E.O.C., 10
Owen, Richard, 55
Paine, C.J., 81
Polignac, Camille J., maj. gen., 45
Randal, Horace, 73
Ransom, T.E.G., 88, 97, 98, 104
Reece, Madison, 77
Rio Grande Expedition, 86, 114
Roberts, John W., 31
Roberts, Oran M., 51, 57, 61, 65
Robinson, Hari, 55, 81
Rowley, Henry, 13
Sayers, Joseph, 43
Sayers, Joseph D., 53
Scott, Reuben B., 13, 60
Seddon, J.A., 73
Semmes, Oliver, 43
Sherman, William T., 37
Skirmish at Bayou Portage, 81
Skirmish at Nelson's Bridge, 35
Skirmish Carrion Crow-Bayou Vermilion, 76
Smith, E. Kirby, 72, 102
Spaight, Ashley W., 19, 29
Speight, J.W., 73
Speight's Tex. Inf. Brig., 19
Spell, Benton, 26, 30
Stillwell, J.L.H., 66
Stone, Charles P., 47
Sweet, Alexander, 110
Taylor, Andrew M., 31

Taylor, Capt. Richard, 92, 110
Taylor, Gen. Richard, 10, 19, 34, 40, 49, 53, 72, 75
Turner, Edmund P., 101
U.S.S. Granite City, 112
U.S.S. Monongahela, 97
U.S.S. Owasco, 88
Ullmann, Daniel, 13
Valverde Battery, 43, 51, 53, 57
Vandever, William, 88
Vicksburg, Siege of, 83
Vidal, A.I., 90
Vincent, William G., 35
Vinson, Bailie, 34

Walker, John G., 12
Walker, William, 19
Walker's Texas Infantry, 41
Waller's Tex. Cav., 19
Warren, Fitz H., 110
Washburn, C.C., 10, 67, 75, 102, 105
Washburn, H.D., 102
Waul's Texas Legion, 83
Weitzel, Godfrey, 10, 43, 63
West, J.A.A., 23
West, Solomon, 30
Wilke, Henry, 106
Willis, John A., 30

ABOUT THE AUTHOR

Michael Dan Jones is a native of Houston, Texas, a graduate of Jesse H. Jones High School and the University of Houston. He served on the *U.S.S. Regulus (AF-57)* in the Vietnam War, the Louisiana National Guard and was a journalist for various Louisiana newspapers until he retired in 2011. He has also been a living history reenactor, taking part in numerous reenactments of battles of the War for Southern Independence. Since retirement, he has been devoted to his church, his family and writing histories of Confederate military units and small battles of the War for Southern Independence. He and his wife, Susan, have three children and five grandchildren.